8-16-18

A Minor Odyssey

Keekee Minor (signature)

KEEKEE MINOR

BAR NOTHING BOOKS
Montpelier, Vermont

A Minor Odyssey

Bar Nothing Books
Capitol Plaza Suite 351,
Box 3, 100 State Street
Montpelier, Vermont 05602
802 223-7086
info@barnothingbooks.com

SAN (Standard Address Number) 256-615X

ISBN-13: 9780976942214
ISBN-10: 0976942216

Library of Congress Control Number: 2016934691

*"The world is a book,
and those who do not travel read only a page."*
—St. Augustine

Table of Contents

Preface—Setting the Stage ix

**Part I Hitchhiking through Europe and the
Middle East 1962–63** 1
In Search of Warmer Weather 3
Egypt Then and Now. 9
An Attempt to Meet My Parents in
the Middle East. 25
Working on a Kibbutz 32
Traveling through Turkey 46
Returning to Europe. 58
Dateline Berlin: November 1963 74

Part II Peace Corps India 1965–67. 93
Applying to the Peace Corps 95
Settling into Worli Chawls 101
An Indian Birth 113
Bombay Heat 120
Ticket Please. 127
Evaluating Success as a Peace
Corps Volunteer. 133
Sikkim: A Himalayan Kingdom 145

Part III Traveling for Work and Pleasure 1970–90 . . . 165

The Reading of Palms and Stars. 167

A Sail through the Bermuda Triangle 175

Keys to Memories. 187

A Changing China. 199

Peace Corps in the Marshall Islands. 211

Reflections 225

Acknowledgments 229

Preface

SETTING THE STAGE

*My father holding me after my
failed attempt as a paratrooper*

My need to move and travel began at an early age.
As a toddler, I would wake up in the middle of the
night, crawl over the bars of my crib, and wander around

the large house where my mother was raised in Steubenville, Ohio. My parents tried to discourage this practice. First, my father, a physician, brought home from the hospital a net that encircled the crib and tied underneath. This approach proved to be no challenge for me. I would flop over the bars, squeeze through the hole in the bottom of the net, and escape. Next, they tried locking the door of my bedroom. That option was also quickly abandoned when my parents found me curled up and shivering against the door. Desperate, they finally put the mattress on the floor, me on the mattress, and turned the crib upside down over me. This early experience exemplifies my innate need to be able to move about freely and discover life on my own terms.

On my second birthday, December 7, 1941, the Japanese bombed Pearl Harbor. My father, like most men of his generation, volunteered to serve. When he was stationed at the Perrin Army Airfield near Sherman, Texas, my mother, sister Mary, brother Howard, and I joined him. After attending an exhibition of colorful parachutes floating gently down from heaven like balloons, I, at the age of three, decided to become a paratrooper. Whenever my mother recounted the story, she always emphasized that I'd used one of her best handkerchiefs to make my parachute.

With four strings tied to the corners of the handkerchief, I jumped from the garage loft. My chute did not open, and I broke my leg in three places. My father took me to the base hospital, where a section of bicycle tire was built into the plaster cast to keep it from slipping when I walked. The story goes that based on the success of my prototype cast, sections of regular tires were then used in the casts of GIs who broke their legs while training to become paratroopers.

Another "footnote" to the experience: A few days after the incident, a neighbor reported that I was crawling around, nude, on the roof of the family car. My mother reportedly asked, "Is she scratching it?"—this an indication that she felt I was quite capable of taking care of myself but was concerned about what destruction I might leave in my wake.

My father was last stationed at Selman Army Airfield near Monroe, Louisiana. There I started first grade. On the days I attended, I found school more than a little boring. For example, everybody was supposed to make letters just like the teacher's. My father seemed to be in cahoots with her. When he showed me how to make a D, I countered with, "That's how my teacher makes hers too, but I make mine like this," and I proceeded to draw a triangle.

My Irish twin, Howard, could not pronounce my given name, Katharine, so he gave me another name: Keekee. In school, when the teacher asked me to spell my name, I decided on the spot that it should have a lot of Es. The name stuck, and my special way of spelling it stuck.

Soon I discovered the art of playing hooky. I would stop off at the playground on the way to school and join up with my classmates when they returned home for lunch. Eventually my scheme was discovered, and at a conference between my mother and the teacher (they did not ask for my input), the decision was made to flunk me.

By the time the war ended, I had lived in numerous places and been shuffled about from one military base to another. After the birth of my younger sister Margaret, December 6, 1945, we moved back to Steubenville, Ohio, where I repeated first grade. I did not like school, ever. The teacher skipped over me in reading because I read aloud so poorly. Everybody but the teacher would laugh at my pathetic attempts. Although the teacher probably thought my ridiculous efforts were intentional and done to entertain the class, they were not, and I was mortified at being exposed.

Reading was not my only problem; spelling was a close second. I lost my battles with teachers when I'd try to negotiate partial credit for words in which I'd gotten all but one letter correct. Society judged me stupid, but deep down I knew I wasn't. In many ways I felt I was smarter than those who were getting A's. My parents accepted my poor grades. I think they knew I was doing the best I could. After looking at my report card, my mother would often say, "They should give grades for imagination. If they did, I'm sure you would get all A's." Two decades later I learned that I was dyslexic, but when I was in school there was no such label.

The ridicule suffered in school was balanced by summers spent in Chautauqua, New York. My parents had spent a weekend there shortly after they were married and immediately agreed it would be a wonderful place to bring children. Toward the end of World War II, my mother wrote to see whether there were places to rent for a week or two. After the summer season had come and gone, she received a letter from the institution stating that there was nothing for rent but there was a place for sale. Buying would have been totally out of the question had it not been that within the same two-week period of receiving that letter, she received an unexpected check that equaled the asking price of the cottage. The check was in payment for an unpaid loan owed to the family bank. When the Depression came, debts were assigned to family members in order to keep the bank afloat. My mother never expected hers to be paid, so when the check arrived, she decided providence meant for her to purchase the cottage, and she did.

As a child I was not so interested in attending the concerts, lectures, and plays offered during the Chautauqua season but instead enjoyed the day camp, where I excelled in sports. No one knew or cared whether I could read or spell, and the positive reinforcement received from my athletic pursuits did wonders for my self-esteem. I thought at the time that since it was a walking community, when I was really old and interested in all the cultural activities it would still be the perfect place to come. Seventy years later, my prediction proved true.

Although it was not a prediction, when I was about eight I fantasized about a program that would not come into being for another fifteen years—the Peace Corps. Steubenville was a town full of immigrants who worked in steel and other mills located along the Ohio River. I was mesmerized listening to all the different languages and would try to imagine where the immigrants might have come from. When I grew up, I thought the perfect life would be to go live among people in some far-off land, teaching them how to live better lives. When the Peace Corps became a reality, I served as a volunteer in India. There I quickly realized that it was I who was the student. It has been the lessons taught to me in the classroom of the world that have added qualitatively to my life.

In elementary school there was a boys' patrol to help direct traffic right before and after school. Thinking it quite unfair that the boys were allowed to come to class fifteen minutes late and leave fifteen minutes early, I lobbied for girls to be included in carrying out this responsibility. I consider the establishment of a girls' patrol at McKinley grade school one of my first organizational successes. Coordinating classmates to drop books off their desks at specific times, and having them bring alarm clocks set to go off at certain times throughout the day, were less laudable agendas but kept me entertained.

The high school in Steubenville was known more for its fabulous football team than for academia, and I went away to school for my junior and senior years. My criterion for selecting schools was not typical. When my mother took me to check out the National Cathedral School in Washington, DC, I rejected it because the halls were too dark; I will never know whether they rejected me. I ended up going to Laurel School in Cleveland. The school was not dark, it was more like an upscale prison where we had little freedom. There I graduated next to last in my class.

My parents, particularly my father, placed a very high premium on education, and so I was surprised when they told me that it was all right if I didn't want to go to college. They were trying to be understanding and supportive, but my gut reaction was that they assumed I would fail. I certainly knew the importance of having a college degree, and when I said I would like to try, they agreed.

My major criteria for college were that it be co-ed and located in a dry climate. (My hair was quite frizzy, and damp weather made it worse.) I ended up going to Colorado College in Colorado Springs. Initially, I thought I would major in math, but I flunked the first semester. I knew the sciences were out because professors teaching in that field had a reputation for taking off for spelling. Since I read poorly and comprehended less, courses in literature were also not options. By default, I ended up majoring in psychology and spent many a night watching rats in cages.

Each semester I made the minimum required grade point for not flunking out. Plowing through words on pages left little room for comprehension, and my painful efforts went unrewarded. Because my auditory memory was superb, I finally figured out that rather than falling asleep in class after staying up late reading assignments that didn't register, I was far better off just getting plenty of sleep, being alert in class, and retaining everything that was said. One professor wrote in one of my bluebooks that it looked like it was written by a third grader; another said I was the most unusual student he'd ever had. I needed a 2-point grade average to graduate, and my senior year, after petitioning to get my average of 1.97 raised to 2.0, I graduated.

I did find time to travel while in college. I spent the summer of 1960 on a farm in Switzerland with the Experiment in International Living before going on to the Olympics in Rome. Memorable trips between semesters included camping at the bottom of the Grand Canyon with the Colorado College Mountain Club—a trip cut short by order of the park rangers, who informed us that the torrential rains we were experiencing in the canyon were nothing compared to the snow at the top, and we were advised to leave immediately. They were right. As we neared the ridge of the canyon, the snow was up to my knees.

Another excursion was with friends to the coastal town of Bahia Kino, Mexico. En route through Guaymas, our car hit a child who had dashed out between two parked cars. Long story, but characters include an ex-con being sought after by the FBI, the American consul, an American scientist, a distraught father, an insurance man, the town mayor (who paid our bail), and the district attorney. The plot included withholding evidence, a court hearing in Spanish that would rival a Charlie Chaplin production, a dead battery discovered after our impounded car was released, a tow over bumpy street roads to recharge it, and our escape to a designated motel near the border, as instructed by the town's mayor.

Although I left the college campus whenever the opportunity presented itself, the excursions, like addictive drugs, left me only wanting more. I knew the need to work would come soon enough, but to reward myself for having slogged through years of academia, I decided to travel until my money ran out. The stories that follow are primarily of travel experienced during this period as well as in the decades that followed. I was never successful at getting the need to travel out of my system, and to this day continue graduate work in the school of international travel.

Part I

Hitchhiking through Europe and the Middle East 1962–63

In Search of Warmer Weather

All packed up and ready to travel

After graduating from college in June of 1962, I worked as a waitress in Chicago for the summer. My life's savings totaled just under a thousand dollars. I calculated this would be enough to travel for a couple of months, maybe more if I was very frugal. The plan was to travel for as long as my money lasted. From my perspective, I had the rest of my life to work, and traveling would give me time to think about what that work would be.

In October of 1962, Abett, Mary, and I boarded the *Queen Mary* and sailed for England. I knew Abett from college, and Mary was a friend of hers from Wisconsin. Our assigned tablemates were three young men, an arrangement I viewed as an auspicious start. We ate together, went dancing most evenings, and often closed the ship's bars. When we docked in Southampton, our brief friendship with them ended—their wives met them.

The plan was to hitchhike to Plymouth, but the first lorry (truck) to stop was headed for Bristol, and so began our pattern of letting rides determine our destinations. Our major priority was to live cheaply so we could travel as much and as far as possible. During our swing through Ireland, we went around the Ring of Kerry on bikes we rented for fifteen cents a day, an expense we deemed within our budget. We generally stayed in youth hostels, but sometimes a driver would invite us to stay with his family. Our driver to Dublin invited us to do so, and in the morning we helped him round up cattle destined for Scotland. A bonus for performing this deed was a free ride on the boat transporting the animals to Glasgow.

We checked off countries as we traveled through them; visiting as many countries as possible became our second priority. It got colder as we traveled through the Scandinavian countries, and we soon found ourselves heading south toward warmer weather. We stopped by London and Paris long enough to visit all the tourist attractions, but weather had become our compass, and we moved on quickly, as though we were running from the law.

In Spain we discovered the weather wasn't much warmer, so on December 7th, my birthday, we left the mainland for the island of Ibiza, where we spent a week defrosting. When we returned to the Spanish coast, we spent a couple of nights in El Campello, a town full of hippies high on drugs and focused on escaping the world. I couldn't wait to leave; I wanted to explore the world, not escape from it.

We scooted further south to Malaga, where we spent Christmas. On Christmas Day I attempted to place a call to my family but gave up after waiting three hours when I learned it would take three days to get my call through.

We wandered around the city in search of places to get warm. Abett was getting restless and decided to return to Ibiza, where it was warmer. Another reason was she wanted to pursue a relationship with a man she had gotten to know there. (I learned months later that the relationship ended when the man's wife chased her away with a butcher's knife.)

After four days in Malaga, Mary and I headed for Barcelona. The weather had yet to cooperate, so we decided to splurge and take a train. It took almost thirty hours, with one stop lasting eight. The many delays were due to snow. Mary and I would get off the train at various stops and throw snowballs. Had we known the stops would be so long, we could have built a snowman. Arriving in Barcelona, we saw a few people venture out into the streets, wearing shiny new boots, and a few cars crawling around the city.

Thinking Italy might be warmer, we made arrangements to stow away on a troop ship destined for Naples. A couple of American sailors, whom we met at a bar, suggested this wonderful plan and said they would make all the arrangements. They took our rucksacks on board two days before the ship was to leave. Mary and I followed the plan, which was to go on board as visitors on New Year's Day. But when we arrived, we discovered our rucksacks were sitting at the end of the gangplank, next to a *No Visitors* sign. Our two sailor friends were nowhere to be seen; in fact, there didn't seem to be anybody around. We made no inquiries but hoisted our rucksacks on our backs and departed for Naples. Although going by boat would have been a nice change, hitchhiking was what we were used to.

A few days later in Nice, France, when we were having dinner with a couple of American sailors, I recounted the tale of our aborted smuggling scheme. They told us that had the scheme been discovered—and they were 100 percent sure it would have been—the two responsible for hiding us would have been court-martialed and more than likely would have spent six months in jail. Not a good outcome.

When Mary and I arrived in Rome, we found lodging in a homeless shelter housed in the main section of an old stone cathedral. In the central area and along the sides there were probably thirty partitioned five-by-seven-foot cubicles, each furnished with a cot. The place was damp and musty and I imagined it contained as many dead bodies as live ones. Marble plaques and figures covered the walls, which towered high above the cubicles. It was downright spooky. In the mornings I was happy to escape to the outside and breathe fresh air. Mary and I wandered around the city checking off all the important tourist sites. Because of cold weather, the sites were not crowded, and we would linger in those that had a little heat.

I spent one day on the back of a motorcycle with an Italian fellow who had just returned from the States after four years. He said that during his stay he had been in a car accident and unconscious for two months. This not-so-reassuring information remained uppermost in my mind as we swerved and sped through traffic. Seemingly the world's worst drivers had all congregated in Rome. I would have advised anyone in similar circumstances to find another mode of travel, but because I had no idea where we were, I did not follow my good advice.

My friend wanted to go to his favorite restaurant, which was on the outskirts of the city. When we arrived, he was astounded to discover that while he was in the States, the restaurant had been converted into a gathering place for Communist Party members. We looked at the walls, which were covered with red-and-black political posters of Lenin and Stalin. Those in the room stared at us, and although I found the experience extremely interesting, the atmosphere made my friend very uncomfortable, so we left. After all, I was just along for the ride.

Fewer youth hostels were open in the winter, and those of us still traveling exchanged information on where to go to get the best rides, what to see, and cheap places to eat. These common agendas served to help form instantaneous friendships and opportunities to travel with others. Mary decided to travel by motorcycle with a fellow she met at one of the hostels. I headed for another hostel in Naples, where I felt confident I would meet others to travel with. As predicted, I did, and they too were interested in finding warmer weather. Within a week six of us found ourselves on a boat headed for Greece.

When we disembarked at the Piraeus Port, near Athens, it was snowing! I had been traveling for three months, and although I'd enjoyed the tourist sights, interesting experiences, and wonderful people along the way, they had all been framed by very cold weather. In desperation our recently reconfigured group unanimously decided to head for Egypt. The night before we sailed, Mary showed up. She had abandoned her motorcycle adventure and, because so many hostels closed in the winter, made an educated guess that I would have gone to Athens. The following morning seven of us traveled deck class to Alexandria, where we hoped we would be able to thaw out.

EGYPT THEN AND NOW

*Campsite for scientists studying Abu Simbel
prior to its being relocated (1963)*

By the time Mary and I reached Egypt, traveling had become a way of life. I found meeting people along the way much more interesting than any particular destination I might have had in mind. I was also fortunate that those I traveled with were easygoing and flexible. We were now eight. Ron, Tom, and Paul were from the Northwest and John and Mike were from New Jersey. On the boat from Greece, another American fellow, Ed, joined our group. Although none of us had any idea of what to expect, we were thrilled to finally find warmer weather when we landed in Alexandria.

Beggars were there to greet us. They were filthy and covered with flies, which they no longer even bothered to brush away. Looking at them almost made me feel clean. As we chatted using the language of charades, one of the beggars informed me that it was too far to walk to any lodging and we would have to take a bus. When I said I had no money, he gave me two piastres. I rationalized that the pleasure it gave him to give me money outweighed my embarrassment.

A bus finally arrived, but with our bulky rucksacks there was no way we could get on. We ended up negotiating a ride in a carriage. Our driver acted as though he was transporting royalty. He waved to everybody we passed and even stopped to put down the carriage cover so onlookers could get a good view of us. Once we found a place to stay, we stored our rucksacks and toured the city on foot.

After exploring Alexandria for a few days, we split up to hitchhike through the desert. Although Mary and I had traveled together through Europe, we decided it would be safer if we each traveled with one of the fellows. I hitched with Paul, and Mary hitched with Tom. The other four took off after we all agreed that we would meet at the youth hostel in Cairo.

Paul and I were fortunate to get a ride with an Egyptian naval doctor, who picked us up because it was his "duty."

When he dropped us at a police stop at the edge of the desert, he instructed those stationed there to find us a ride. All cars were stopped, even when it was clear that there would be no room to take us. A couple of times we had to push cars to get them started again.

We finally got a ride, and not just any ride, but one in a 1959 Ford! It was very plush, with carpeting and a radio. While traveling along in this luxury, we spotted Mary and Tom trying to thumb a ride at the side of the all-but-deserted road. Paul asked the driver to stop, but the driver said he didn't want to pick up any more hitchhikers. When Paul explained they were our friends, he relented. As they were getting into the car, the driver asked Tom if he had a gun and was surprised when he said no. He told us we were naive; it was dangerous to travel through the desert without a gun. I wasn't quite sure whether a gun was needed for snakes or people.

We stopped at an oasis, where our driver treated us to a delicious meal of steak, hummus, yogurt, bread, and grapes. When we arrived in Cairo, he took us directly to the pyramids. Paul and I rode camels, and the other two rode horses. There were no other tourists around. I felt very special. It was as though we had the whole desert to ourselves and the pyramids were there to greet us.

Our driver then dropped us at the youth hostel, which was fairly central and served as a good base. Children often followed us as we wandered around the city. They were very friendly and clearly enjoyed trying out their extensive

English vocabulary of "hello" and "OK." But when I tried to take a photo of some of them playing in a schoolyard, their attitude changed and they started throwing stones at me. I later learned that many Muslims believe it is a sacrilege to have their pictures taken. Only Allah creates, and trying to duplicate what Allah creates could lead to idolatry. It made me wonder about the justification for all the pictures of President Nasser displayed in shops, restaurants, and almost all public places.

When I visited the Museum of Egyptian Antiquities, the place was filled with original artifacts that I'd only seen pictured in schoolbooks and *National Geographic*. As I walked through the museum viewing the remains of ancient history, I was again surprised that there were so few tourists.

We went to the American embassy, where a staff member provided us with historic and useful information, including a heartfelt warning that under no circumstances should we swim in the Nile. She said the river hosted liver flukes, parasites that could kill us.

For a change of pace, literally to rest our feet, we went to see the American film *Elmer Gantry* for ten cents, and for a bit of nightlife we decided to visit Desert City. I understood it to be a collection of a few tents where belly dancers performed, a nightclub of sorts, with performances taking place in tents out on the desert. Mary and I accepted an invitation to go with a medical student we'd met. We traveled by taxi out to Desert City, where she and

I had arranged—and fully expected—to meet up with our fellow travelers. This did not happen.

We did go to a tent, but it was not in the neighborhood of any other tents, which made me a little suspicious. It was decorated with bright red carpets, three beds, stools, and colorful pillows strewn around the interior. There were a couple of men in the tent when we arrived, but I saw no belly dancers. At first it wasn't clear to me what the entertainment would be, but I soon found out it was drinking, and smoking hashish. I hadn't smoked hashish before but agreed to give it a try.

It wasn't long before I started seeing things through different eyes. I became mesmerized staring at the three lonely pyramids backlit by the moon and silhouetted against the desert night. At the time I thought, "it can't get any better than this," but then realized that if Mary and I didn't leave soon, it could get a lot worse. We could easily become the primary entertainment. I told her that we were leaving immediately and to get into the taxi, which had waited. We jumped in, locked the doors, and instructed the driver to take us to the youth hostel.

The story didn't end there. When we got to the hostel, Mary and I told the driver we were unable to pay and he should have collected the payment from our "date." Needless to say, given our speedy departure, there was no way this could have happened nor, given the circumstances, would our date have been happy to pay for our escape. Altered states of mind do not always give the most reasonable reading of a situation. Our driver seemed to accept the explanation and left.

The warden (manager) in charge of the hostel poked his head out of the second-story window and said he would only let us in if I promised to go out with him. While unproductive negotiations were going on, our driver, unbeknownst to us, had gone to the police station to file a complaint. He returned shortly with two policemen. The lodging problem was solved as Mary and I spent the night in jail.

When we arrived at the jail, I was wide-awake and in a festive mood. The policeman in charge asked if I wasn't concerned about causing an international incident, which was the least of my worries on a long list of no worries. When the phone rang, I asked whether it was Nasser calling and if he was going to be joining our little party. I broke into song and truthfully thought I sang as beautifully as, or possibly more beautifully than, anyone I had ever heard. Mary later told me that she too thought my singing was exceptional. Proof that drugs alter one's perception.

After my performance I sat on the bench between Mary and the poor taxi driver, who appeared a little bemused. He gave Mary and me part of the meal his wife had packed for him. I thought of it as an indoor picnic.

Having given the medical student's business card to the policeman in charge, we all waited for him to be tracked down so the driver could be paid and we could be released. It was almost dawn when the money arrived. The taxi driver excused himself, and we parted friends.

Mary and I decided to stay until it got a little lighter but left abruptly when one of the policemen tried to take her purse when she nodded off. She snatched it up, and we both marched out. No one tried to stop us.

The streets were deserted as we made our way back to the hostel. Because staying at the hostel was no longer an option, our group packed up and moved out; that afternoon we were given permission to stay at a government campsite.

Although travel in Europe often evolved with destinations determined by where a driver was going, in Egypt some planning was necessary. After researching various options, we all agreed we should go check out Abu Simbel, the site of two temples that had been cut into sandstone cliffs during the thirteenth century.

Getting there involved going partway by rail. We were told to take the train to some town; I didn't know the name of it, but somebody in the group did, and from there we were to take a bus to Aswan. When we arrived at the train station, it was packed with people pushing and shoving, and almost immediately the eight of us became separated. Unlike our gentlemen friends, Mary and I were unable to squeeze onto the train. Catching up with the rest of the group was essential, as Ron had my rucksack, Paul had the water-purifying pills, and most importantly, we weren't exactly sure where we were going.

Mary and I did make the next train, and when we got to the next station, I spied Paul, John, and Mike through the window. They too had missed the train but had taken a taxi to the next station in hopes of catching it. They had decided to wait for the eleven o'clock train as it had first class but confirmed that Ed, Ron and Tom had made the first train. Fortunately I remembered to ask where we were to get off: the end of the line.

Mary and I spent most of the ride talking with Hussein, an engineer who was working on the Aswan High Dam. Through conversation with him and his wife, we learned that they had four sons and a daughter, Princess, who had been given the honor of presenting flowers to Marshall Tito, the president of Yugoslavia, when he came for an official visit. They insisted, and we agreed, that we would stay with them when we returned from Abu Simbel.

When we got off at the end of the line, we found ourselves in the middle of nowhere. The only structure was a dilapidated bus stop, and perched in the tree next to it was Ron. He was shirtless and bearded and reminded me of an oversized monkey.

We were thankful not only to have our little group puzzled back together but also that we made it in time to catch the daily bus to Aswan. Every seat was taken, and the roof was piled high with baggage. Most of the men wore what looked to me like pajamas, a practical and comfortable fashion more prevalent in the countryside than in the city.

Once we arrived in Aswan, we booked deck class on a supply barge headed for the Sudan. At night, lined up on the deck in our sleeping bags and sheltered by a starlit sky, we took turns picking out the various constellations. I slept well but woke up feeling a little shaky and queasy. Because there really wasn't much I could do about it, I just carried on.

We moved up the Nile slowly and docked, or rather ran aground, at various stops along the way. It was hard to spot landing sites as the banks of the river varied little. An irrigated strip of green bordered the western bank, but the eastern bank was desert. The docking procedure consisted of tying our two connected barges to a tree. People would then trickle in from various directions, collect supplies, and disappear back into the desert.

The scenery varied little, and when Abu Simbel appeared, it looked like a fake backdrop. Dwarfed in front was a collection of tents housing geologists and other scientists charged with analyzing how Abu Simbel could be elevated and moved back from the river. If no solution was found, the temple would be submerged under the Nile when the Aswan Dam was completed. Looking at it, I could not imagine that such a feat would be possible.

So there were the temples, and there were the people studying them; that was it. Although we had originally planned to stay a couple of days, it was clear the place would not hold our interest for more than a couple of hours.

I walked around in a daze, feeling worse every minute. I was light-headed and dizzy and realized that, in addition to off-and-on bouts of dysentery, I might be having sunstroke. My face was bright red, hot, and swollen; I looked for shade, but there was none. An old Arab, noticing that I was in trouble, invited me into his tent. I was resting on the ground when Tom poked his head in and announced the group had decided to continue on to the Sudan.

Back on the barge, my friends located a cabin that had an extra bunk; it was there that they stored me for the next couple of days. I was young and assumed I would live, or maybe I was too sick to realize I might die. Day and night ran together, and I slept my way back to health in the dark cabin as we moved gently up the Nile.

I was back in the land of the living by the time we reached Wadi Halfa, and after setting up camp on the bank of the river, we took a swim. So much for the good advice the embassy staff had given us. In the evening we heard drums in the distance. Following the sound to its source, we discovered a festive celebration in process. We were invited to join in, and soon we were all gyrating to beating drums, clapping hands, and laughter. It was a black-and-white scene. The Sudanese were very black, and their skin contrasted sharply with the whites of their eyes and gleaming white teeth. Many of them had never seen white people at close range, and women approached me, touching and rubbing my face and arms.

Puffs of dust danced around moving feet, and chants rang out across the desert. Periodically old women would

pierce the night sky with sounds of high-pitched ctt ula-
tions. It was in this isolated surreal setting that I became
acutely aware that wherever I was in the world, I would
always be with myself. That night, snuggled in my sleeping
bag a few feet from the Nile, I stared at the stars scattered
across the sky and replayed the memory of the evening
before drifting off to sleep.

In the morning Mary and I met Koko, a man who offered
to take us across the Nile in his felucca. Within minutes we
were sailing swiftly to the other side of the river. When we
reached it, Koko pointed to a shelter in the distance. At
first the straw structure was hard to see because it was the
same color as the sand. Walking was slow and difficult. We
hadn't gone far before we were hit by a sandstorm. I had
seen movies of sand storms and therefore knew what one
looked like, but could not have imagined they could be so
painful. The sand felt like thousands of needles shooting
into my skin; I wanted to cup my eyes in my hands to protect them. The sand penetrated everything, through my
clothes and into all the crevices of my body. Mary fell to
the ground and covered her head and ears. She struggled
to get up when Koko and I approached her. The three of
us trudged on toward the makeshift straw hut owned by
Koko's friend, Mohammad.

The hut reminded me of the story of the three little
pigs. It had four straw walls, a straw bed, and a straw table
and chairs. The straw house of the three little pigs had
blown down, and I wondered whether this house would

survive the storm. Mohammad, looking magnificent in a flowing white caftan and stark white turban, made us tea while we all waited for the storm to abate.

As was our pattern, we stayed for only a few days in the Sudan, never venturing far from Wadi Halfa. Because the village would be covered by water once the Aswan Dam was completed, plans were underway to have it moved inland.

When we returned to Aswan, Mary and I kept our promise to the couple we'd met on the train to Aswan. Hussein and his wife greeted us with genuine enthusiasm and immediately made us feel part of their family. It was Ramadan, and some family members followed the practice of fasting from dawn until sundown. One of the sons chose not to, while another, who would have been excused because he was ill and spent most of the time in bed, was determined to observe the fast. The religious observance also exempts children, so Princess, the daughter, was excused.

At sunset, the daily fast ended. We enjoyed a substantial meal—interrupted by family members who disappeared for prayers, food, and to greet drop-in friends. After dinner Hussein, an engineer, took Mary and me to the construction site of the Aswan Dam. Work on the dam was done at night, not only because it was cooler but also because needed power could be diverted from Cairo for the project's use. The Soviet Union had a significant role in the construction of the dam. Because it was during the Cold War, a time in history when Russia and America were not on the best of terms, I wondered what the Russians working on the project might be thinking as Hussein showed us around.

I don't remember much of what he told us, but I do remember thinking he might be telling us more than he should. It was a mammoth project, and I knew someday I would have to return to see for myself the engineering feats of both Abu Simbel and the Aswan High Dam.

*   *   *

That someday came in 2010, almost fifty years later, when I returned to Egypt with the National Press Club. An Egyptian bodyguard traveled with us, as required by the American embassy. The historical sites that had been around for eons were still there, but the footprint of the ancient culture seemed to have been lost in the sand and replaced with the business of tourism. Buses were everywhere, transporting batches of people from fancy hotels to the pyramids, museums, and mandatory souvenir shops. Egyptian guides corralling tourists reminded me of nomads shepherding goats. My memory of being made to feel so special during my first visit was replaced with the reality that I had become a commodity.

But even as a commodity, I was able to appreciate the efforts being made by Egyptians to preserve their past. Abu Simbel had literally been raised to new heights. The temple, which I remembered as a dark and cavernous room, was crowded with tourists on walkways. Lights revealed much of what I had not seen before, including rooms that branched off from the main room. The outside remained as impressive as ever, and although I searched for signs of trauma, which might have occurred when the structure was raised and moved further back from the Nile, I found none. Although Abu Simbel looked the same, I was not able to recognize the site where the Aswan Dam now exists.

On this same follow-up trip, I had the opportunity to take a ride in a hot-air balloon. Our group was staying on one of the many hotel boats docked at Luxor, and the two of us who had opted for the excursion left at about 3:30 a.m. in order to be in time for liftoff at dawn. We were given a lesson on how and where we should sit when we landed. These precautions had been instituted because of a fatal accident the year before. The company had been required to discontinue operations and only recently been given permission to resume flights.

The pilot assured me we would not be bumping into any planes; they stayed on one side of the Nile, and the hot-air balloons stayed on the other. We flew over many houses where the top floors were exposed to the sky. It seemed most were used for storage, but some had chickens or other animals wandering around. TV satellite dishes were everywhere. I felt like a voyeur as I peeked into the lives of those below me—children playing, shoppers wandering through colorful markets, traffic jams, life in progress.

When it came time to land, we couldn't. There were too many telephone wires in the way. When I overheard the pilot call on his cell phone to explain that we would have to land on the other side of the Nile, I was thrilled. It meant that our excursion would be extended by at least another twenty minutes. We floated over Luxor Temple and hotel boats sitting patiently on the banks of the Nile. In the distance we had a wonderful panoramic view of the Valley of the Kings. As we landed gently on green, irrigated farmland, crew members arrived in a chase vehicle to help passengers out of the basket before they deflated and packed up the balloon.

I was delighted to have had the excursion unavoidably extended, but those waiting outside the bus when we returned were less enthusiastic. They knew the delay was not our fault and understood that being part of a group has both advantages and disadvantages.

As I age, I've come to appreciate many of the advantages. I have adjusted quite nicely to sleeping in a comfortable bed rather than a sleeping bag, and I appreciate eating food that is unlikely to make me sick. Having someone else worry about logistics and transportation falls somewhere in between. Although I am happy to delegate the worry factor, I dislike being herded like cattle from one place to another, and sticking to a predictable itinerary of sites to be visited is less appealing to me than letting experiences percolate up randomly. I miss chatting with drivers who picked me up during my hitchhiking days.

Their stories interested me more than listening to a tour director rattle off facts and statistics about various places. But age dictates that if I am to travel, I must adapt.

In a world that is changing at an ever-increasing rate, I have learned to appreciate the historical perspective my life has given me—the special moments of both the then and the now, and in particular those moments that tie the two together. On my return trip in 2010, I met an old man whose son was the owner of a perfumery we were obligated to visit. When I learned that he had grown up in Wadi Halfa, I pulled out a photo I'd taken of the barge I'd traveled on in 1963. He said he remembered it well; it was the barge that brought supplies to his village before it was moved inland. He asked if he could have the photo. I said, "Yes, that's why I brought it."

AN ATTEMPT TO MEET MY PARENTS IN THE MIDDLE EAST

While traveling in Egypt, I received a letter from my parents saying that they were planning to take a Mediterranean cruise. The ship would be docking at Haifa, and they wondered whether I would be able to meet them. I lost the letter, and couldn't remember the name of the ship, but I was pretty sure it started with the letter *M*. The date of their arrival was also a mystery, but I was fairly certain it was sometime in March. In today's world, I would just go to an Internet café and Google ships cruising the Mediterranean in the month of March, but fifty years ago there was no such option. Being a lucky traveler, I decided to leave the possibility of connecting with my parents in the laps of the gods.

After thawing out in Egypt, I, and the remnants of the group I'd been traveling with, left Alexandria on February 23rd and headed for Lebanon. Upon landing, Mary and I accepted a ride from a fellow who said that for religious reasons, it was his duty to buy us clothes and take care of all our needs for three days. I did not for one minute think his ultimate intentions were of a "religious" nature, but taking risks, which depended primarily on cost and other available choices, was just part of my life as a hitchhiker. Because I wanted to see Beirut, and for me it is always more interesting to see a place through the eyes of a local, we accepted his offer.

As we drove along the Mediterranean Sea, with its many different shades of blue, our driver recounted the time in 1958 when over five thousand U.S. Marines landed on the beach—everyone had been taken by surprise, including some who were sunbathing. Late in the afternoon, we drove up a tightly terraced hillside and stopped at a small restaurant for a delicious meal and a wonderful view of snowcapped mountains. As the sun was setting, I asked our "good shepherd" if he would please take us to the youth hostel. Although he appeared to be asking for directions from those in the restaurant, I was not at all surprised when he told us there was no youth hostel in the area. With a straight face, he went on to explain that he wanted to be true to his commitment and suggested we stay at his brother's. The game was now moving in the anticipated direction.

When we arrived at his brother's, a party was in the making. We were introduced not only to his brother but also a few of his male friends. By then it was dark, and even though I knew it was going to become one of those tricky situations, we stayed. It was clear that other options would not be offered. I was much more interested in sleeping than in partying. The bouts of dysentery I'd suffered in Egypt had returned, and I felt totally drained. When the brother showed Mary and me the room we were to occupy, it took me about two seconds to jump into bed with all my clothes on and another ten seconds to go to sleep. Later, I was abruptly awakened when Mary came in and quickly locked the door. After the pounding on the door subsided, I slept fitfully until about five the next morning, when Mary and I stealthily climbed out the window and escaped.

We met up with Mike and John at the hostel, which turned out to be walking distance from where we'd stayed. The following morning, the four of us left for Damascus: I traveled with Mike, and Mary with John. Because there was no such thing as a cell phone, we depended on luck to reconnect.

The person in charge of the hostel in Damascus had been a tour guide, and since we were the only ones staying there, he took us all over the city to see the sights. Our special treatment included drinking tea from china cups as we sat by the cozy fireplace in the hostel kitchen. It would have been nice to stay longer, but we left after three days. I was anxious to get to Jerusalem in hopes of figuring out when my parents might be arriving in Israel.

We discussed various vague options of where to meet when we reached the Jordanian side of Jerusalem but committed to none. Too much planning could become stressful.

Mike and I ended up staying in a filthy place where I counted fourteen snails or slugs crawling around the sink that was past the possibility of ever being clean again. The creepy-crawlies moved slowly, and I was able to gingerly wash my face without coming in contact with any of them. Going to the bathroom was a balancing act, requiring me to stand carefully on slimy, mossy footprints. I wore boots to give me traction so I wouldn't slip and fall into the unimaginable. Although youth hostels weren't fancy, places like these made them look upscale. The next day Mike and I changed our lodging, and within a few days we reconnected with Mary and John.

Over the months, I was lucky to join up with like-minded travelers, those who focused on eating, sleeping, seeing the sights, and moving on. It was the credo of most students traveling at that time. Little did I know that in four months' time, I would end up hitching in Spain with a fellow who knew Mike from New Jersey.

After a couple of days, Mary, Mike, and John moved on. I stayed and found lodging at a convent located on the outskirts of Jerusalem. A taxi driver in the area who said his name was John—so that's what I called him—would drive me into Jerusalem in the morning and bring me back in the evening.

Jerusalem's cobblestone streets, whitewashed archways, and timeless buildings reminded me of biblical pictures I'd seen as a child. Some men wore Western-styled clothing, but the majority of both men and women dressed as they had for centuries.

John helped me locate a travel agency. Putting the pieces together, I guessed that my parents might be on a ship that included an optional side excursion to a museum located in the Jordanian section of Jerusalem. Even though the possibility that my parents might be on the excursion was only a guess, I registered to cross from Jordan to Israel on two different days. (Travelers were required to register three days in advance to cross from Jordan to Israel.)

There was a conflict the morning the museum tour was scheduled. John, without consulting me, had made arrangements for a photographer to take my picture. At first I said no, as I was afraid I would miss the tour group, but I finally agreed because he had been so helpful. The delay did make me miss the tour and, helpful or not, that was the end of John.

The woman at the museum had no idea whether my parents had been with the group, which I had missed by half an hour, but she was sure the group would have already departed by plane for Beirut. According to the information I had collected, the ship was due to depart from there and head for Haifa the next day. I was glad I had registered to leave on two different dates.

My frustration at having missed the tour group was mitigated by my bumping into three of the fellows I'd met in Egypt. Although Jerusalem tended to fold up early, which I presumed was due in part to Islam's prohibition of alcohol, the fellows had discovered the Hinky Dinky Bar, which is where we celebrated our last evening in Jordan.

The following morning, as the four of us walked through the Mandelbaum Gate and meandered slowly toward the Israeli section of Jerusalem, I observed men from both sides watching us from behind sandbag fortifications draped with barbed wire. In Europe most border crossings had been perfunctory to the point of being almost meaningless, but the crossing into Israel was significant. I had the feeling I was walking two centuries into the future, leaving behind a biblical setting and arriving in a modern world. Experiencing the time warp gave me a rush of adrenalin, and all of a sudden life seemed sharper.

Although I went to great lengths to collect entry and exit stamps, I didn't have my passport stamped when entering Israel. An Israeli stamp in my passport would have prevented me from being able to enter an Arab country in the future. Keeping my options open was more important than the extra stamp.

Once inside Israel, my friends and I parted. I made my way to the bus stop, and although I missed the last bus to Haifa by ten minutes, I was able to make a connection through Tel Aviv. When I arrived in Haifa, I immediately headed to the port. Boarding the ship I had decided my parents must be on, I asked to speak with the purser. He was emphatic that my parents were not on the ship. I pleaded with him to recheck, but he insisted he was not mistaken. Clearly he wanted me off the ship as soon as possible, and I have to admit that my appearance, which included my father's full-size World War II army rucksack, did not fit in with the ambiance of the setting. I could see from the glances of passengers that they too would like to see me off the ship. I agreed to leave. I was disappointed, but knew I had done my best, except for maybe losing the letter with the information containing the ship's name and itinerary.

Just as I reached the gangplank, I spotted my parents descending the steps from an upper deck. They were alone. Had they walked down those steps a minute later, I would have been gone. The purser had convinced me that they were not on the ship, and I had already made up my mind that I would not return.

They were ecstatic to see me and had no idea of how close we had come to missing each other. We had a good visit and I was able to spend the night on the ship, which meant a hot shower and good food. My parents sailed the following day, and I stayed behind to go work on a kibbutz.

I have thought many times of how close I came to missing my parents. It felt as though my guardian angel was showing off special skills, ones in addition to those she used to protect me from danger. (I admit I kept her pretty busy, and when she went off duty or took a well-deserved vacation, I did sometimes get into unfortunate situations.) But on the day I connected with my parents, one could say she was spreading her wings.

Working on a Kibbutz

The State of Israel had been established fifteen years before I arrived in March of 1963. Individuals and families were emigrating from countries around the world to help build the new nation. I wanted to make my own contribution by working on a kibbutz. It would not only be an opportunity to experience history in the making, but after five months of traveling, I also needed to feel useful.

When I picked up my mail at the American Express in Haifa, I learned from a message left for Abett, whom I had traveled with initially, that friends of hers were working on Kibbutz Ein Hamifratz. I headed there and met the fellows who had left the note. Ein Hamifratz had a number of student travelers and others who had come to work for a short time. Although they were at capacity for accommodating foreigners, I was able to spend a couple of nights there before returning to Haifa and going to the Israeli Student Tourist Agency (ISTA) to see about getting placed on another kibbutz.

At ISTA, I met a woman from Kibbutz Ga'aton in western Galilee. She had stopped by the office to visit with a friend working there. We talked briefly, and she explained that although Ga'aton was not organized to take many outsiders, if I wanted to return with her I could work there. Why not, I thought. We left a few minutes later, and when we arrived at Ga'aton, she asked Lallie, a Canadian girl who was leaving in a few days, to help me get settled. On our way to collect clothes issued by the kibbutz, Lallie explained that whereas Ein Hamifratz was larger and had an established student program, Ga'aton at that time had only four "students" (all foreigners were called students). She said little effort was made by members of the kibbutz to include those coming from the outside, adding that no one would talk to me but not to take it personally. I doubted this but would soon learn that she was more right than wrong.

After collecting my work clothes and toiletries, Lallie took me to my lodging—a freestanding small room with magazine pictures tacked to faded blue cardboard walls, a cement floor, and a single light bulb hanging from the ceiling. There was a cot, a stool that I could use as a table, and two outlets, but of course I had nothing to plug into them. Later I was issued a hot plate on which to make tea. Having adjusted to sleeping in hostels, where dormitories precluded privacy, I was delighted with my new living space.

My friend of a few hours and I went to dinner, which consisted of chicken, a variety of vegetables, yogurt, and fresh bread. We sat on wooden benches with others who conversed among themselves. Many knew German, but few used it, and those who did were shunned. Members wanted nothing to do with Germany. I was told that when three German students arrived to volunteer their services some months before, they were asked to leave immediately. The rationale given was that their fathers might have been members of the SS, implying the students might have inherited some genetic disposition to be like their fathers. I assumed the students had probably wanted to help heal the wounds inflicted by Hitler's Third Reich, but the hatred toward Germans could not be so easily erased.

There was a heaviness about Ga'aton, and although I was not privy to the internal politics, I could sense there was an uneasy alliance between those members who had been there for some time and newcomers arriving from various countries. Life on my kibbutz was very structured, and although it seemed to suit those who had been incarcerated in concentration camps, others complained it was too structured.

The community would arise at 5:30. Outside, and a few yards from my room, was a spigot where I would go to brush my teeth and wash my face. These morning ablutions were performed on a carpet of colorful flowers as the sun rose; it was a wonderful way to start the day. Everyone worked for a while before breakfast, which was served in shifts from either 8:30 to 9:00, or 9:00 to 9:30; at meals there was always more eating than talking.

Work assignments, as well as leadership roles, were rotated so members could experience all aspects of the community. There a few exceptions. Because the future of Israel depended on its children, teachers and caretakers primarily responsible for raising them received special training and were not part of the general work pool.

Another exception was Shmuel Katz, one of the founders of Kibbutz Ga'aton and a well-known artist. I was told his housing was nicer than anyone else's, but no one minded because the income from the sales of his work was passed directly on to the kibbutz.

The last exception I was aware of was Joel, who had held the position of sanitary supervisor for the previous six years. He told me he had been one of 1,500 out of 6,000 who had escaped from a Hungarian concentration camp and that he had lived underground in the Warsaw sewage system for four years during World War II. He had been at Ga'aton for eleven years. I learned from others that although he fantasized about leaving the kibbutz and moving to Nahariya or Haifa, each time he attempted to do so he developed psychosomatic symptoms and had to return. After four attempts he finally gave up.

Like most people on the kibbutz my jobs varied, but I mostly washed dishes. When people handed me their plates, there was little eye contact. I learned quickly that my Canadian friend had been right, but I didn't mind being left to my own thoughts and was content to just observe.

One day, and it turned out to be literally one day, I was assigned to work in the laundry. As soon as I walked in,

I knew I was not welcome. My cool reception was from a close-knit group of women who had known each other at Auschwitz. The numbers tattooed on their forearms told me they had painful stories I would have been interested in knowing, but I knew I never would. They made me feel incompetent and corrected the way I ironed, telling me that I should do the collars and sleeves first and then the bodies of the shirts. I tried to follow their instructions but knew that even if I ironed perfectly, they would still not want me around. Like many others on the kibbutz, they chose to isolate themselves.

Another work experience was in Ga'aton's small industry, which made nuts and bolts. My job was quality control. If the hole in one of the nuts was not centered, I was to reject it. The work was tedious, and I kept thinking trained pigeons could probably do a better job. Still I came to appreciate my meditative existence. Because I was all but ignored in most settings, I was surprised when one day, as I left the factory, a Hungarian couple approached and asked if they could speak with me. They were older, and I didn't even remember seeing them in the dining room, let alone the factory. Of course I said yes.

The couple wanted to thank me for coming to work on their kibbutz. They were embarrassed that they, and others, did not befriend me and felt I deserved an explanation. Because they had lived in concentrations camps during World War II and suffered the loss of so many friends and relatives, they had no emotional reserve to make friends with those they knew would be leaving. It was too painful. They hoped I understood. I did.

When assigned to work in the orange grove, I had the opportunity to meet Israelis who were not members of the kibbutz. In Israel, when one turned eighteen, he or she was required to serve in the army: two years for women and two and a half for men. Young women picking alongside me said their six weeks of basic training included a ten-day rotation at Ga'aton. After the first six weeks they would either work for the government or stay in the army for the balance of their two years.

Although no one was allowed to wear makeup on the kibbutz, some of the female recruits, as well as kibbutz members who had emigrated from Latin America, obviously spent a good bit of time styling their hair. Others clearly thought such an activity was foolish and a waste of time and energy. The differing opinions, between those who had lived on the kibbutz since its inception and the more recent arrivals, created low-level tension.

Working outside in the orange grove was wonderful. The air was clean and invigorating. The ground was an artist's palette of blue, purple, red, yellow, and white flowers that grew wild between the rows of orange trees. I would cringe when the horse-drawn cart collecting the fruit would come through and crush the flowers, destroying my giant flower box.

When the workday ended at 4:30, community members relaxed and visited with friends. It was also the time, between 4:30 and 7:00, when children were able to be with their parents. The structure for raising children started at birth, with the mothers and newborns staying in the hospital for four days. The newborns were then moved to a nursery, where their mothers would go to feed and spend time with them.

After six weeks, the mothers gradually returned to work. Specially trained teachers and nurses were primarily responsible for raising the children. Although there was general agreement on how they were to be brought up, some members were concerned. Because all essential items were issued, children were growing up without understanding the concept of money. Some members worried that when the children became adults they would be at a disadvantage in the outside world. Others, who wanted the children to remain on the kibbutz throughout their lives, did not see this as a problem.

Kibbutzim were socialistic communities where money never seemed part of the culture. When my Bolivian friend Ed, from Kibbutz Ein Hamifratz, came to spend the night, I'd wanted to purchase a bottle of wine. My request created a lot of confusion because there was no system for charging me. After two days of discussion, the leaders decided to just give me a bottle.

During my six weeks on the kibbutz, I never needed money. On one occasion, I had to see a dentist in Nahariya. An appointment was made for me, and I was transported with others in one of the community vans. It was my first experience with socialized medicine. Like those with me, I was given a number and asked to wait. After a while, I was given another number and moved to another area. I ended up getting a gold crown, which I have to this day.

If someone wanted to go into Nahariya or Haifa, he or she could get a ride in the community van. I appreciated the convenience of reliable transportation and took advantage of this service a couple of times. Once I missed the return vehicle from Nahariya and decided to walk back. It was the start of Shabbat and therefore there was no traffic. The only moving thing I saw was a snake swishing across the road. That was a little scary, but the fact that I was not sure where I was going was not. I had been walking for hours when I arrived at a *moshav*, another type of communal settlement.

I asked how far it was to Ga'aton and was told that not only was I going in the wrong direction, but if I kept going, I would end up in Lebanon. The members were friendly and helpful. They provided me with food, lodging, and conversation. I learned that in a moshav community, members raised their own children, farmed their own land, and did not have communal dining. The feel of the place was lighter and inviting, quite different from the controlled structure of Ga'aton. Even so, the opinions expressed were similar to those I'd heard elsewhere in Israel. They were disappointed in American Jews because they were first Americans and then Jews. A cartoon in the *Jerusalem Post* stated that emigration from the States had increased by 100 percent from the previous year: two Americans had arrived.

When they learned I'd traveled through Egypt, Lebanon, Jordan, and Syria before coming to Israel, their interest shifted from the States to my impression of those countries. I think they were hoping I would have some political insights. I didn't. But I told them that the Arabs, like them, had been friendly and hospitable and had been curious about my thoughts on Israel, which at the time I had known even less about. It was a refreshing couple of days, and on Monday a driver headed to Nahariya gave me a lift to Ga'aton—a significant detour, but he seemed happy to do it.

Although it wasn't part of the culture, I liked the idea of having a little money to buy things. One time, after picking up my mail in Haifa, Ed, my friend from Ein Hamifratz, and I each sold a pint of blood for eight dollars. He had a relatively rare Rh-negative blood type and tried to negotiate for more money but didn't succeed. After donating, I didn't drink anything, and as a result I almost fainted in the middle of the street. Ed found me a place to sit down in a shoe-repair shop and explained to the owner that I was pregnant (I wasn't). The shop owner was very attentive and concerned about my possible needs. I revived quickly after Ed returned and gave me a bottle of orange drink.

Each time I returned to the kibbutz after a day in town, I became increasingly aware of how excruciatingly predictable everything had become. Each month, rations of coffee, jam, tea, toothpaste, and other staples were distributed. The menu was always the same. If we were having chicken, I knew it was Friday. I had no reason to complain, as all my basic needs were being taken care of and any extras would have been considered extravagances. Because my brief exchanges with community members were generally limited to work and logistics, I felt I was becoming intellectually stagnant.

In May I went into Haifa to watch the Independence Day parade. It was a military parade, with tanks moving through the streets and planes zooming overhead. I thought to myself, "There is no way all these boy toys are not going to be used." The parade generated an excitement around me that made me realize how flat my emotions had become. So with my mind becoming stale, my emotions becoming flat, and my spirit wilting, I knew it was time for a change.

Carol, an American girl who had arrived at Ga'aton a few weeks earlier, decided to join me on a swing through Israel. We were told that since we had been working on a kibbutz, we could stay on others for free. This was not the only good news; we found hitchhiking to be very easy. Drivers were required to stop and pick up military personnel wanting rides, and those in uniform often volunteered to flag cars down for us.

The travel rejuvenated me. As I moved back into the world, layers of ignorance were peeled away by experiences.

Although the mechanics of living on a kibbutz seemed to vary little, I learned there were differences. A member at one kibbutz I stayed at asked me about my political affiliation. I was confused by the question and wasn't sure what he meant. He pointed to the white string tie laced into my kibbutz-issued royal blue sailor shirt and told me it signified the Mapam political party. For weeks I had had no idea that my dress was announcing a political affiliation. He had no trouble believing my ignorance.

Each time I stayed on a kibbutz, I learned a little more. It surprised me when I was told only one kibbutz was Orthodox, although maybe it shouldn't have since many Israelis said they were not religious and thought of Judaism more as a culture. Some admitted that when they had lived elsewhere, it felt both culturally and religiously important to follow a kosher lifestyle, but once they arrived in Israel, their homeland, it was no longer necessary.

There were pockets of traditional living. I unknowingly stopped for lunch at a kosher restaurant in Safed. The proprietor said that he could not serve me a hamburger and a milk shake; I could order one or the other but not both. I ended up getting a hamburger at that restaurant and then going across the street and ordering a milk shake. Although Safed was known for its art, I remember it for its food.

Hitchhiking proved to be very easy. Sometimes more than one car would stop to pick us up, and often drivers were more interested in chatting than in getting to their destinations. But our luck seemed to have run out when we got to Be'er Sheva around dusk. We'd hoped to get a lift to Eilat, but there was zero traffic. A passerby, guessing our predicament, informed us that trucks could only travel in caravans at night. He pointed to a nearby truck stop and wished us luck.

We went over, and although none of the drivers had planned to go any farther that evening, there were soon four trucks making their way across the Negev Desert. The first thing our driver did was pull out a gun and put it on the dashboard: "Protection," he said. This frightened Carol, who immediately sat on the floor of the cab. She spent a cramped, uncomfortable night there while the driver and I enjoyed a spectacular drive through the desert. There was nothing but sand, and a sky sparkling with stars, with no ambient light to spoil our view. Our little caravan made its way through the magical desert and arrived at Eilat at dawn. I had been given the name of a retired army general, and although it was 6:30 in the morning, we found his place and knocked on the door. Despite the early hour, he welcomed us and, over coffee, expressed his frustration on the never-ending fighting occurring in the Middle East.

After sleeping on the beach a couple of nights, Carol and I returned to Be'er Sheva in different trucks. There was no caravan requirement during the day, but the road was almost as sparsely traveled as it had been during the night. After miles of no traffic, my driver spotted a truck in the distance and just stopped in the middle of the highway.

At first I wasn't sure what was happening, but when the driver in the oncoming lane also stopped, I knew they must be friends. Both drivers jumped out and embraced each other, and there in the middle of the highway, in the middle of the desert, the two proceeded to chat away. After a few minutes my driver motioned for me to get out. He introduced me to his friend, who then got back in his truck and left.

Because we were already stopped, my driver asked me if I'd like to shoot his gun. I thought, why not? He placed empty soda cans on the sand dunes, and we took turns firing at them before getting back in the truck. It was then that he told me we were only a couple of miles from the Jordanian border! Two thoughts: one, if I had known that, would I have taken up his offer to shoot, and two, was the border just a line in the sand?

When I returned to Tel Aviv, I purchased a ticket on a ship due to leave for Turkey in a few days. My total number of rides for the eleven-day excursion through Israel was forty-eight. My lodging included four kibbutzim, one truck, two pensions, the beach in Eilat, and two nights with Israeli families. It felt good to be back on the move again.

For many, the structured life on the kibbutz worked well, and I was glad to have had the opportunity to experience it. The two and a half percent who chose to live on a kibbutz gained satisfaction from knowing that they were making essential contributions to Israel's survival as a nation. They grew food not only for their community but also for those living in the cities. Some kibbutzim were strategically located to protect the country's border, and many of them established small industries to supplement income and foster independence.

I have always found living in other cultures educational, but my experiences in Israel were special because of that particular time in its history. It was no longer in its infancy but a toddler learning to walk. One could already see that in adulthood it would be strong and productive. I was glad that in my own small way I had had the opportunity to contribute to its development. But it was time for me to move on. I returned to Ga'aton, collected my things, and left the following day. I was excited as I boarded a boat for Turkey to embark on my next adventure.

TRAVELING THROUGH TURKEY

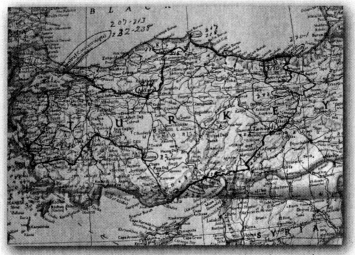

*Map of Turkey showing my route and number of overnight
stays, beginning and ending in Istanbul*

I sailed from Haifa to Istanbul on May 14, 1963. The boat docked for an afternoon at Cyprus because traveling directly from Israel to an Arab country was not permitted. I equated the stopover with being quarantined for a few hours. While in port, a Turkish fellow gave Anne, a Canadian girl I met on the boat, and me a tour of his part of the island. His analysis of the ongoing political disputes between Turkish and Greek Cypriots was understandably biased in favor of Turkey.

Once back on the boat I met another Turk, who asked if I would mind taking one of his bags through customs in Istanbul. He wanted to avoid paying duty and said the bag contained a bathing suit and a couple of women's blouses. I thought of it more as doing a favor for someone than of doing something wrong—like smuggling. The good deed became complicated when customs detained him. I waited, but when he didn't show, I left.

A few days later he tracked me down at the Nur, a quirky little hotel in Istanbul known for housing student travelers. He didn't tell me why they had detained him, and I didn't ask, deciding he probably wouldn't tell me the real reason anyway. By then I had checked the bag to make sure that my "good deed" had been limited to transporting only clothes. I gave the bag to him, and he disappeared from my life.

That evening, Anne, my new friend from the boat, and I went to a chai house for dinner. The place emptied abruptly, leaving us, and a couple of armed soldiers. The soldiers explained there had been a coup of some sort and a curfew was in effect in Istanbul, Ankara, and Izmir. They suggested that for our own safety, they should walk us back to the Nur. I was glad for our military escorts, as the streets were dark and deserted.

I was also glad news did not travel instantaneously, as it does today. While I always knew I was fine, my parents would have worried if they realized I was arriving in Turkey just as a coup was taking place. I did send them postcards and letters fairly frequently but was sure by the time mail reached them, and they figured out where I'd been, the coup would be old news. My mother saved my letters and postcards, and reading through them decades later I found them to be as bland as I had intended them to be. Parents don't need to know everything.

Living off the grid gave me a sense of freedom. Why would anyone want to be inundated with communication overload from the Internet or in constant contact with others by cell phones? These inventions would have distracted and interfered with my being able to live in the present, followed by space and time to absorb and reflect on what I was experiencing.

The Nur, a one-star or maybe two-star hotel, was a good place to meet others with similar objectives. There I met Muryl, another Canadian. She, Anne, and I decided it would be safe, or safe enough, if the three of us hitchhiked together. After having our fill of looking at mosques and wandering through the bazaar, we headed towards Sinop, a port city on the Black Sea. Hitchhiking proved to be a challenge. There was very little traffic, and with three of us each carrying oversized rucksacks, I am sure potential drivers thought twice, or maybe three times, when considering whether to offer us a ride.

On our way to Sinop we met a couple of Peace Corps volunteers from the first group serving in Turkey. I definitely had planned to join the Peace Corps but had felt I needed to travel before settling down in one place for two whole years. The two Peace Corps volunteers, as well as those they introduced us to, were flabbergasted that we were hitchhiking. I don't recall seeing any other hitchhikers, let alone female hitchhikers. I had the feeling they equated us with aliens dropping in from outer space.

Near one village we had a five-hour respite, eating and drinking with a Turkish garrison in a grove of shady trees. One of the soldiers read our fortunes from coffee grounds. My diary contains no reference of what he predicted—probably that I would travel a lot. Then, as now, I realized that I could never have these unique experiences on an organized itinerary.

We took a bus on the last leg to Sinop. The distance was 162 kilometers, about 100 miles, and although we left at 9 a.m. we did not arrive until 7 p.m. We stopped numerous times for tea, twice for gas, twice to check the tires, and a couple of times to take pictures. Periodically we picked up and dropped off passengers waiting alongside the road.

When we got to Sinop, it didn't take us long to learn that U.S. army personnel were stationed there. Although we were told the area was highly restricted, we walked right in. The GIs stationed there referred to Sinop as "the end of the world." It might have seemed so to them but not to me. I enjoyed the treat of a hamburger and an ice cream sundae and was thrilled to be able to buy a soap dish and notebook at the PX.

Sinop was, in fact, an out-of-the way place. Had we looked at a map, we might not have chosen it as a destination, but we were glad we did. Our lodging was only fifty cents a night, and the GIs went out of their way to make us feel welcomed. One of them made arrangements to have the man who had come to fix the air-conditioning system stay over a day so we could get a ride with him, and another threw a party for us.

The air-conditioning man took us as far as Samsun, and from there we got a ride from a man who recognized me from the bazaar in Istanbul, where he owned a shop. When he said he was going to Trabzon and that we could go with him all the way, we jumped at the opportunity. Unfortunately the roads were very bad, so we stopped in Giresun overnight. He told us we should be ready to leave at seven the following morning.

We were up in time, but the shop owner and his driver had already left. I didn't blame them for sneaking away early, as we were a lot of extra weight. It had rained steadily overnight, and while we were debating what to do, Anne looked out the window and saw a man preparing to leave in the one lone car sitting in front of the building. We ran down and asked the driver, who was German, where he was headed and if he would have space for the three of us. It turned out that he too was going to Trabzon, and he agreed to take us.

We didn't bring him much luck either. The roads were in dreadful condition. We stopped once to change a tire and numerous times to get out and push the car through swollen riverbeds. We got totally lost and ended up in a place so isolated that teachers let their students out of school to come stare at us. Our driver was agitated and seemed frightened about being so lost. Only later did he tell us that we had drifted into Kurd territory, where, by reputation, the people were hostile to outsiders. Thanks to my ignorance, I had not been frightened and had found the curiosity of those we stumbled upon understandable.

Just how lost were we? Well, it took us fourteen hours to drive what should have been less than a hundred miles. We eventually arrived in Trabzon at about 4:30 a.m. Our exhausted driver disappeared, and we never saw him again. We too were exhausted and slept most of the following day. We budgeted for food and lodging but not time.

On Sunday, June 2nd, we started off again. We would walk a while and then rest. Perched on my pack, I enjoyed sitting and looking at rolling green hills with backdrops of snowcapped mountains. The expansive uncluttered landscape gave the country a masculine feel, reminding me a little of Scotland. It was the antithesis of Switzerland, a manicured, well-groomed, feminine country. Although hiking a few miles and soaking up spectacular views were wonderful ways to pass the time, we were thankful to finally get a ride in the back of a truck transporting people and a couple of cows.

The views continued to be magnificent, but the aroma, courtesy of the cows, was off-putting. The truck stopped when a man at the side of the road waved it down. We passengers looked on, as the business of selling the animals took place. I got the feeling it might have been prearranged. There was much hand pumping, which ended when the two cows started to wander off. No one in the truck was disappointed to see them go. As we pulled away, I watched as the buyer scurried after his new acquisitions. When this particular ride was over, the driver jokingly asked for my camera in payment.

By definition, hitchhiking provides unique experiences. If you are part of a group, you assume that the driver of a bus has credentials and that the tour leader knows, and follows, an organized itinerary. But not so when hitchhiking. The itinerary doesn't much matter, but you hope that whoever is in the driver's seat is skilled. This was particularly true in Turkey, where roads, huddled against the mountainside, were treacherous. The ability of some drivers was iffy at best, adding to the thrill—or, in some cases, terror—of a ride. If a vehicle dropped over the side of the road, its passengers would go straight to eternity. My rides proved to be worth the gamble, and although I survived to tell my tales, there were accidents.

One bus driver swerved around a curve and smashed into an old man and his cart. Everybody piled out to have a look. The man's face was streaming with blood, and his body looked like a pile of rags. Splinters from his cart flew everywhere, and strewn around him were all his worldly possessions: a box containing tin utensils, an old shoe, a weathered notepad, and threadbare clothing. I could easily have believed the scene had been there for days and disintegrated over time.

A couple of passengers placed stones to preserve the skid marks; another passenger went over to the old man, opened one of his eyes, and blew into it to see whether there was a response. Eventually someone put a blanket over him. An hour or so later, a lonely truck arrived. I cringed as I watched the old man being carried off in a jumbled fashion, each step diminishing a little more of any life that may have been left in him. No one knew who he was. No one faulted the driver. The old man had just been in the wrong place at the wrong time.

Passengers were slowly plucked from the highway by passing trucks. Around two o'clock, a busload of Iranian students offered us a ride. After boarding the bus, we discovered it was bound for Trabzon, the place we had just left! Not wanting to retrace our steps, we hopped off the bus and went back to sit in the sun and wait with the remaining passengers.

A few minutes later, one student returned to say they were changing their route in order to take us. Since we were going in an entirely different direction, maybe they, like us, didn't have much of a destination and were just traveling around Turkey. I don't know who was more excited about the change of plans, them or us. They bombarded us with questions about America and Canada and were eager to soak up our firsthand information about places they had only heard about through the media.

Since the bus was full, three of the students volunteered to stand so we could sit. I was watching the road more closely than the driver, who kept looking at me in the rearview mirror. I tried changing seats a few times, but every time I did, he just adjusted the mirror. His lack of attention to the road was disconcerting to say the least, and I was relieved when we had to stop because of a landslide that covered and blocked the road. Who knew how long it would take to clear? Although the Iranians had to wait until the road would become passable, Muryl, Ann, and I didn't. After thanking them, we climbed over mud and rocks and caught a ride on the other side, in a vehicle that had had to turn around.

The miserable weather returned, and after traveling through a tremendous hailstorm, we decided to take refuge in the next town. We located an overcrowded tearoom but were stopped at the door. Females were not allowed. The men instructed us to go to another entrance of the hotel, but we pretended not to understand. After much lively discussion by those inside, someone came out and informed us that permission had been granted for us to enter. I gather we were the first exception they'd ever made. After all the hoopla, I was amused that when we finally entered, the men vied for our attention, each insisting that we sit at his table.

Although we were tired and had become sopping wet while waiting, once we entered the tearoom, time slipped away. We eventually excused ourselves and made arrangements to spend the night at the hotel, which cost each of us twenty-five cents. It was a sleazy place. Men leaning against the wall leered at us when we went down the hall to the bathroom.

After putting a chair against the door, we bedded down for the night and promptly fell asleep. But it wasn't long before we were abruptly awakened. Loud voices accompanied pounding on the door. It was our Iranian friends. The landslide was cleared, and they had succeeded in getting through. We needed to hurry and leave right away: the bus was waiting.

There was no electricity, so we frantically fumbled around in the dark feeling for our belongings, rushing as fast as we could so we wouldn't be left behind. Not a chance. All the students were waiting for us outside the bus. As soon as we were all settled in our seats, excluding the three volunteer standees, the police arrived. The police said it was too dangerous, as everyone needed to be in a seat. We were ordered off the bus.

I was not all that disappointed. There was the darkness, the inattentive driver, and roads that were hardly passable. Even I thought we were pushing our luck a little too far. I was glad my guardian angel, in the form of a policeman, had come to our rescue.

We got off and returned to our room, only to find that our beds had been reoccupied! It didn't take us long to get rid of the men who had replaced us in our beds; after all we had paid for a night's lodging! The sheets hadn't been clean to begin with. Maybe bedbugs and lice had been added to the mix, but it didn't matter, we were just happy to have a dry place with walls.

We were up at five and on the road shortly thereafter. During the morning we made great progress, but after lunch our wait was more than three hours, with only two trucks passing us. Walking seemed a bit futile, so we sat on our rucksacks in the beautiful setting of nowhere. Finally a third truck, transporting gravel and some fruit, picked us up. Due to my vivid imagination of what could happen, it turned out to be the most frightening ride I ever took.

We traveled through the spooky night, with only dim headlights to guide us through the fog. We stopped to pick up a driver from one of the two trucks that had passed us earlier in the day. I didn't see the truck he'd been driving, but my imagination assumed it must have gone off the cliff. There was no traffic. I found myself shaking with fear, thinking that at any moment we would go flying off the cliff and into the depths of blackness below. During the day I could at least see the edge of the road and the valleys that stretched into the distance. In the eerie darkness I could see nothing. We stopped once at about 3:30 to deliver vegetables, which gave us a little more space on the pile of jagged gravel.

We reached Adana at 5:30 a.m., alive. Muryl had become very ill with bronchitis, so we immediately set out to find ourselves a hotel that had clean sheets and no bedbugs. After a couple of days, Muryl felt better. We made our way to Konya, stopping once to enjoy the beach at Mersin.

There was a certain rhythm to our rides. Not only did we stop for passengers, gas, and flat tires, but depending on the time of day, we'd stop so devout Muslim men could pray. They would get off the bus, spread a small prayer rug on the ground, take off their shoes, and lie prostrate in prayer. Given the scariness of some of the rides, I was happy to have prayers said!

At a truck stop in Konya, we met the driver of the truck from which the two cows had been sold. It felt like a reunion of old friends. Reconnecting after many miles and many days, he announced to everyone in the establishment that he had asked me for my camera in payment for our ride. The room filled with laughter. We had shared a unique experience defined somewhat differently. For him, it was picking up three girls hitchhiking in Turkey; for me, it was having two cows sold out of the truck in which I was riding.

Anne left us in Izmir to go stay with friends she had met on the boat from Haifa. Muryl and I returned to the Nur Hotel in Istanbul. Daily, we would go to the Hilton Hotel and order a pot of tea with refills of water. As we elegantly sipped our tea, we discussed where we'd like to go next. Why not the Running of the Bulls in Spain?

RETURNING TO EUROPE

*Muryl and Keekee trying to hitch a ride at the
border between Turkey and Greece*

After traveling for a month in Turkey, Muryl and I
zipped across Europe in time for the Running of
the Bulls in Spain. My interest in the event was prompted
by Hemingway's book *The Sun Also Rises*. I only read it
because it had been a class assignment. As a dyslexic, I
tend to read to have read something, rather than for the
enjoyment of reading. Plowing through a bunch of words
resulting in minimal comprehension was not my idea of

a good use of time. But then if I hadn't read the book, I might never have gone to Pamplona for the Running of the Bulls.

Muryl and I stayed at a campground packed with student travelers from all over the world. It was located fairly close to the bullring, the destination where both bulls and runners would be headed the following morning. The runners would get a head start, and their primary objective would be to get to the bullring before being trampled to death.

We left the campsite early the next morning so we could locate a spot with an unobstructed view. Although I was squashed up against the barrier bordering the running path below, I could see perfectly. I heard the cheering crowd and the sound of trampling feet moments before the runners came into sight. Dust clouds quickly soiled the runners' traditional white clothes, accented with bright-red neck scarves and red sashes tied around their waists—items worn to attract the attention of the bulls. As they ran past me, faces filled with panic and determination, it was clear they knew the risk they were taking. That year four men lost their lives, including a father of four.

The bullfights were in the afternoon and I quickly learned that fans were not shy about expressing their feelings. A packed crowd displayed their dissatisfaction with the performance of the up-and-coming matador El Cordobes. They threw garbage and seat cushions at him, which I thought was a little harsh and not very sportsman-like, but I have to admit the crowd's explosive energy added to the experience.

Camped near our tent was another Canadian, Jean, who had a car! She wanted company, and we wanted dependable transportation. Within a few minutes, we decided not only to travel together but that it was time to move on and collect a few more stamps in our passports. We headed to Gibraltar by way of Portugal. On our way to Lisbon, we had three flat tires, and another one on our way from there to Gibraltar. So much for dependable transportation.

We had only just arrived in Gibraltar when I realized I had food poisoning from what I assumed was spoiled shrimp. Although periodically I was not in the best of health, I seldom thought of myself as being really sick. This time I was. Looking at me, Muryl knew it was serious and proceeded to stop the next car coming down the street. The driver, Victor, graciously agreed to take me to the hospital, and when I was released, he arranged for me to stay at a pension for a few days.

I recovered quickly and after a week decided an excursion to Tangiers was in order. Morocco would give me another stamp in my passport, and scooting across the Strait of Gibraltar would be an experience in itself. I didn't know what to expect but was surprised by what I found. Tangier seemed to be the mecca for drugs. In Egypt I had smoked hashish, but I had little knowledge of other drugs.

The Central Café seemed well named, serving as a primary location for arranging all kinds of drug deals. There I met a collection of interesting characters. The one I spent the most time with was Alan, referred to by the regulars as the English Watchmaker. He was a cheerful young man, who casually told me that his passport was being held as collateral until drugs he had arranged to be shipped to England arrived safely. He would then get his passport back and be paid $300. (I was told by friends years later that he ended up in jail.)

Customers ordered drugs like drinks. On a rooftop overlooking the city, I ordered hashish. While I was under its influence, mesmerizing music played in the background as I fixated on the city spread out in front of me like a priceless painting. My senses became sharper, colors seemed more vivid, and sounds more beautiful. Shifting focus to my hand, I watched it quietly move around in the air. Life and time flowed slowly with no concern for the future or past...there was only the pleasant present. I could easily understand how and why people become addicted.

When I witnessed the effects of some of the more potent drugs, I wisely chose not to try them. Totally incoherent patrons using these drugs stumbled around and looked ridiculous. I wondered whether they had any idea of how they appeared to others. Maybe they were in some sort of zone they enjoyed, but I doubted it. To me, it looked as if their only agenda was to escape. Not all trips, as they are referred to, are positive. Looking at them, I knew I did not want to go to wherever their trips were taking them.

One morning, at about 5 a.m., I decided to go look at the sunrise. I was carrying a book somebody gave me: *The Rise and Fall of the Third Reich*. Books were recycled through the traveling community, and although I knew I would never get through it, I thought I might read a few pages before passing the book along.

At that early hour, some people had just gone to bed, while others were just getting up. Only a few roamed the streets. A man seeing the book I was carrying became excited and insisted I wait where I was, on a corner in front of a café. He returned a few minutes later with a record player. He just happened to have a record player with him. That was the first thing I had a hard time believing. The second thing was that he proceeded to put on a record of Nazi marching songs, turning the volume up as loud as he could! Soon a few Arabs gathered around the player and began gyrating enthusiastically. It was all I could do to keep from laughing at the incomprehensible scene taking place just as dawn was breaking.

I assumed that because of the swastika on the cover of the book, the man took me for a Nazi sympathizer. I asked him nothing, but he jumped right in, explaining that he had been a lieutenant in the German army and claimed he was present when Hitler shot himself. He'd spent five years in a Russian prison camp and was now living in Algiers for political reasons. He went on to tell me that he had written a book on irrigation. He was loquacious and eager to share all these details with me. I just listened. I knew that after the war, Nazis scattered and hid themselves around the world, but I never thought I'd meet one. When I left, I think he still believed I was a Nazi sympathizer.

Although during the day people were involved with making drug deals and sobering up, the nights were reserved for partying. People drank and smoked their drug of choice. There was dancing, which was more like prancing around to music; some looked as though they were acting out the definition of how an idiot would behave. Alan and I would go from bar to bar. I made sure my experimenting with drugs was limited. But even as an observer, I realized that an extended stay in this environment would not be good for my body or soul. It was time to leave.

When Muryl and I checked our funds, I discovered that I'd been robbed of almost all my money, which at the time totaled approximately $7. An Indian shop owner overheard our conversation and gave me $2 so we could book our return passage. I asked for his address so I could send him the money. He requested that I send it to his wife in India. The address was on Girgaum Road in Bombay, and a few years later when I became a Peace Corps volunteer stationed in Bombay, I lived on that same street. At that time I attempted unsuccessfully to locate the family to see whether the money had ever arrived.

Returning from Tangier, Muryl and I searched near the port for a car that had Gibraltar license plates. We located one and waited to see whether we could get a lift from the driver. He arrived shortly and said he would be happy to take us, but he warned that there might be a delay at the border. He was transporting a prisoner who had been in a

Spanish jail for over a year for smuggling transistor radios. The prisoner was nineteen and quite cute. We didn't mind at all and jumped in.

When we reached the border between Spain and Gibraltar, the border official did not question the driver or the recent prisoner. Instead, he leaned in and asked me how much money I had. I explained I had been robbed in Tangiers and had the equivalent of about 50 cents. The border official ordered me to get out of the car. "I told you one day you'd be sorry, and today's the day," he sneered. I suddenly realized that it was the same man who ten days before had propositioned me while I was waiting on the beach in Gibraltar for friends. When I had turned him down, he had warned me that one day I'd be sorry.

I wasn't concerned. I asked the official if I could use the phone to call Dick Reeves, a commentator for the local radio station, as Muryl and I were to be interviewed by him that evening. Not surprisingly, the official seemed to assume that I was making this up. He dialed the number and handed me the phone. I explained to Dick that the interview could not take place because we were being detained at the border. He asked to speak with the official, who, after a brief exchange, grudgingly said I could go, providing I left Gibraltar within twenty-four hours. Muryl and I swung our rucksacks onto our backs and walked across the airport tarmac, which served as the border divider between Spain and Gibraltar. I knew I would be able to stay in Gibraltar as long as I liked. I had connections.

Actually I had one connection, Victor, who had come to my rescue when I first arrived. He was well known and respected by everybody. I knew that once I was back in Gibraltar, he would make the necessary arrangements to have me stay as long as I liked.

Staying was not a problem, but money was. By this time Jean, who had declined the Tangier excursion, had gone off on her own. Muryl, who had already been traveling for five years when I met her in Turkey, decided she would stay and work for a few months, make a little money, and then move on. Because she had done an astrological reading for Dick Reeves during our radio interview, she was able to get a job doing readings in a local tearoom.

Unlike Muryl, I planned to travel for as long as I had any money. Actually, I was fresh out of money, but I had a few rations given to me by members of the Royal Air Force based in Gibraltar. I figured the rations would be sufficient to get me to Madrid, where I expected to have money waiting. I had written my parents asking them to withdraw $50 from my bank account and send it to the American embassy in Madrid.

The morning I left Gibraltar, I got a ride with a man who was on his way to pick up his daughter at camp. He was concerned about my hitchhiking alone and said he would postpone picking her up until the following day. He ended up taking me all the way to Madrid. It was 3 a.m. when we arrived, and I asked him to drop me off at the American embassy. He waited to make sure they would let me in.

The marine on duty accepted my excuse that it was too late for me to go to a hotel and allowed me to sleep on a couch in the reception area. At 10 a.m. I realized it must be Sunday because no one had come to waken me. Another marine was on duty, and I asked him to check to see whether I had any mail. I didn't. I asked him to check again as I was out of money and was pretty sure my parents had arranged for some to be sent. Nothing.

Knowing I needed a place to stay for a few days until money arrived, he suggested the university in Madrid, where, during summer months, girls were permitted to stay. He insisted on giving me 200 pesetas. I didn't want to take it, but he said he'd only use it to buy beer.

After four days of waiting and still no money, I decided I needed to move on. (I would learn weeks later that my parents had driven to Alaska and hadn't gotten my letter.) The person responsible for running the university hostel didn't charge me. He knew I was waiting for money that hadn't arrived.

I hit the road and headed for Verdun, France, to visit Jane, a friend from college whose father was the commanding general at the base there. While I was waiting for a ride, another hitchhiker suggested that we hitch together. We chatted while waiting, and it turned out that he knew Mike and John, who were part of the group I'd traveled with in the Middle East. Such a teeny, tiny world.

After a couple of rides, we split. He headed towards Burgos, and I continued on to Verdun. I was lucky to get a ride for two days with a family of five (with children aged 1, 3, and 5). They had a camper, and at night I slept next to it. When they dropped me off the next evening, they gave me approximately $2 in French francs, enough for a night's lodging at the youth hostel.

I was a little less lucky the next day. The first driver who picked me up was not really interested in taking me toward my destination, and my intuition told me I should get away from him as soon as possible. When he slowed down, I opened the car door to get him to stop. He did. Within a matter of seconds, I'd jumped out of the car and yanked my rucksack from the back seat. He looked stunned. He sped off, leaving tire marks, indicating he probably wasn't too happy. I was relieved.

My last ride that day was with a GI based in Verdun. He initially was willing to take me to the address I gave him but reneged when he realized it was the home of General Grothaus. Maybe he thought he might get into trouble if he deposited a rather forlorn-looking traveler on his commander's doorstep. But I found my way easily enough, as the general lived in the tallest house in Verdun.

The family received me as though I were their prodigal daughter finally returning home. My menu of rations was replaced with home-cooked meals, accompanied by fine French wines. I enjoyed and appreciated hot showers, clean sheets, and a comfortable bed, all luxuries I had learned to live without.

When I arrived, I could sense there was a bit of excitement churning in the air, and I soon learned why: Jane was going to marry a GI named John Kearns in November. She asked if I would be her maid of honor, and of course I said yes.

The wedding wasn't for a couple of weeks—enough time to squeeze in another adventure. Jane lent me money to purchase a bike at the PX, and after a week of being thoroughly spoiled, and assuring her mother that I would be back in time for the wedding, I left. My plan was to travel along the Meuse River through France, Belgium, the Netherlands and then return via Germany. There was a towpath alongside the Meuse, so how could I get lost?

On the afternoon of my first day of biking, I stopped to ask a woman working one of the locks how much farther it was to the Belgian border. The woman tried to explain that I was on the outskirts of Saint-Mihiel, a town south, not north, of Verdun! When she pointed in the direction I had just come from, I laughed. She was sure I hadn't understood and ran to get a map. As a dyslexic, I have never been good with directions, nor do I have an aptitude for languages, but I had clearly understood what she was trying to tell me.

I turned around and retraced my steps—or, in this case, my pedals—back to Verdun. Later, General Grothaus asked me if I'd thought about looking at the sun to figure out which direction I was going. I said I hadn't but that it really didn't matter. My fifty-mile mistake had been a beautiful one, with spectacular fall foliage lining the towpath. After resting a day, I started off again, this time in the right direction.

Because I didn't know I was supposed to have a permit to travel on the towpath, those working the locks proved to be very helpful. They would alert me to the location of police checkpoints, so I could detour around them. I would bike for hours without seeing anyone and amuse myself by counting the number of times I pedaled per kilometer. Biking for me was a meditative experience and the exercise a plus.

There were only two incidents in my travels when I was truly frightened. One was the time in Turkey when I was riding in the back of a truck that I feared might go over the precipice at any moment. The other was when I needed to trek across meadows at dusk with my bike. I kept moving, lugging the bike over barbed-wire fences in hopes of finding my way back to civilization. The animals roaming in the meadows were probably all cows, but because I had recently been to the Running of the Bulls in Spain, I kept imagining that at least some of the animals were bulls preparing to charge me. Imagination is a wonderful thing, but not all that bubbles to the surface of consciousness is positive.

It was dark when I finally reached a road. The light on my bike was powered by pedaling, and it took all my diminishing energy to keep the bike moving. Fortunately a town and lodging were not far. I was exhausted when I arrived and thankful I had survived my imagination.

With winter approaching, fewer students were traveling, and many youth hostels were closed. On my way from Antwerp to Rotterdam, I stayed at the hostel in Bergen op Zoom. The quiet, woodsy location fit its storybook name. Actually, it was very quiet, as I was the only one staying there.

As I approached Rotterdam, I was impressed with an underwater tunnel constructed just for bicycles. There were also red and green bike lights at traffic intersections. Cyclists were confidently in charge of the roads. I quickly learned not to make eye contact with drivers, as they would expect me to move out of their car's way.

I loved biking, but when the terrain shifted from almost flat to uphill as I headed toward Germany, it began to feel more like a chore. When I got to close to Düsseldorf, I talked with a couple of barge captains about getting a lift, or in this case a float, up the Rhine. Jose agreed to take me. He was Dutch and claimed to have made the most runs on the Rhine the previous year. The only crew member was a boy of about fourteen, who helped with tying up and casting off. We decided I would be the cook.

We left in the afternoon and docked at Cologne about 8:30 p.m. The city reminded me of Steubenville, where I had grown up, along the Ohio River. I disembarked, and although I intended to stay at the youth hostel, it was too far. Jose wanted to keep his record of the most runs on the Rhine for another year and had asked me to be back on the barge and ready to leave by 6 a.m. I ended up staying at the homeless shelter in the train station. Many noisy children were also staying there, but I was tired and went to sleep immediately. I woke up at 4:20 a.m. It was still dark when I reached the barge a few minutes before 6.

I found Jose curled up on the floor next to the potbelly stove. (I learned later that day that the bulk of the cargo we were transporting was whiskey and thought that maybe after I'd left the night before, he had decided to sample a little.) He was pleased to see me and got up quickly. Learning that it had taken me so long to get to the barge seemed to concern him more than it did me.

Our conversations took place with the help of charades. He understood English more than I understood German, but we managed to communicate, or pretended that we did. If the translation wasn't quite right, it didn't much matter.

We docked early in the evening and tied our barge to another one already in port. Those working and living on the barges made up a self-contained community and, except for me, everybody seemed to know each other. Jose and I climbed from one barge to another, visiting residents in the defined neighborhood. A boat arrived with supplies and Jose bought coffee, potatoes, and pork chops. One of the neighbors explained that most of them seldom went ashore, as all essential items were brought out to them.

That evening though, Jose said he needed to go into town for an errand.

I cooked while he was away and made enough potatoes to feed a dozen. I never said I could cook. When Jose returned he seemed pleased with himself. I discovered that his errand had been to go out and buy new sheets and linens for me. He showed me one of the two cabins on the barge and said it was to be mine. This way I would not have to worry about getting back for our early-morning departures. He made it clear that he would not come and bother me; the cabin was to be just for me.

The next few days were filled with beauty. Brightly colored foliage lined the banks of the river, and sometimes I would spot a castle high up in the hills. Again I was reminded of Steubenville and other towns along the Ohio River, where barges filled with coal, iron ore, and manufactured goods used the river for transport. There were no castles along the Ohio River, but both scenes gave me the feeling of life meandering slowly along a waterway.

Although I would have preferred to stay on the barge a few more days, I had a commitment: Jane's wedding. I told Jose I would write him, and the following spring, during my three-month teaching career, I had my third-grade students do just that. He in turn sent each of them a picture postcard, thereby introducing geography into the curriculum.

I arrived back in Verdun in time for the wedding, much to the relief of Jane's mother. It was a spectacular affair, with seven U.S. generals stationed in France and Germany attending. After the ceremony, the bride and groom went off on their honeymoon, and I was again free to move on.

The loan from Jane was dwindling, and I was again almost out of money. Because my thirst for travel and experiencing different cultures had not yet been quenched, I decided it was time to return to the States and apply to the Peace Corps. But first I needed to go to Berlin.

DATELINE BERLIN: NOVEMBER 1963

*Soldier patrols section of the Berlin Wall located
in front of the Russian War Memorial*

"We thought you were an East German trying to escape," the interpreter responded. I had asked him why East German soldiers had snatched me off the autobahn at gunpoint as I walked from the outskirts of Berlin to the checkpoint. Had I made it to the checkpoint, my chances of getting a ride all the way to Hanover, in the western part of Germany, would have been excellent. Because the autobahn from Berlin ran through East Germany, no one stopped along the way by choice.

"Didn't anyone see that I had an American flag hanging over my rucksack?" Even as I said this, I knew it was a weak retort. He said nothing. As the minutes ticked by, the questioning became more of a conversation. I was curious and so asked, "How many Americans have you picked up?"

"None," he said. "You are the first one." His statement jolted me, and in that moment the enormity of the situation in which I found myself crystallized.

President Kennedy had been assassinated on November 22nd, ten days before, and the world was in a state of shock. During stressful and dangerous situations, I tend to withdraw, observe, and stay cool. Following Kennedy's assassination, I felt that I had been successful in distancing myself from the emotional impact others seemed to be feeling, but the comment by the interpreter of my being the first American they had picked up produced a torrent of butterflies in my stomach.

I had been hitchhiking throughout Europe and the Middle East for fourteen months. My itinerary had evolved as I traveled. Nobody suggested Berlin as a destination, but I thought that because it was always in the news, particularly since Kennedy's "Ich bin ein Berliner" speech, it was as good a place as any to round out my adventures before returning to the States.

This last leg of my travels had started in Munich, and it was there that I learned of Kennedy's assassination. The day after his death, instead of hitching to Berlin as planned, I went to the American consulate, a magnet for those of us not quite sure what to do. I waited in line with businessmen, tourists, and students to sign one of the many memorial books. The mood was one of unsettling disbelief.

The rest of the day I spent meandering around the city, collecting newspapers and magazines. I didn't know German, but the pictures under the headlines needed no translation. Those who guessed me to be American would invariably ask, "What will happen to the wall?" Why they thought that I, at twenty-two, could give them a rational explanation baffled me. Nevertheless I reassured them, as much as myself, that there would be a smooth transition of power and there was nothing to fear. My programmed explanation, delivered from a calm exterior, hid the apprehensive thoughts that raced around my mind on a track with no finish line.

The next day I trudged to the outskirts of Munich to hitch a ride to Berlin. My father's army rucksack weighed heavily on my five-foot-two-inch frame. The American flag draped over the pack had proved helpful in getting rides from drivers who fought in WWII, and I reaped the gratitude they felt toward American GIs as I listened to their stories.

Eighteen years before, at the end of the war, the spoils of Berlin had been divvied up between East and West. During the two years just previous to my visit, the Russians and East Germans had built a wall to prevent those in the East from escaping to the West. America's relationship with Russia was far from ideal, and therefore I found it ironic that my last ride to the East German border was with a Russian couple. We were unable to communicate verbally, but I interpreted the lift as an expression of condolences.

At Hof, three German students returning to the University of Berlin gave me a lift. The boys rearranged their books and bags to make a place for me in their well-traveled VW Beetle. After we introduced ourselves, they didn't talk much but instead focused their attention on calculating time and mileage. They explained that it was forbidden to stop on the autobahn and that if we arrived too soon, they would be questioned about speeding. If we arrived late, they would be asked why we were delayed, where had we stopped, how long, and why. I sensed they'd learned this from experience. I was tired and glad I did not have to engage in idle conversation to earn my ride. While the car radio played classical music in the background, I meditated on the trees colored by fog, which clicked by with the rhythm of the car.

We were stopped at a checkpoint, asked to show our passports, then instructed to get out of the car and go to a small building, where I was questioned about how much money I had. Since only paper money could be exchanged for other currency, I'd saved loose change from dozens of countries. My collection of coins clattered onto the counter as I dumped the coins from my purse. Although I found it amusing that the officials took such undue interest in what I considered Monopoly money, I kept a straight face and shrugged every time they held up a coin for me to identify. My hidden amusement quickly subsided when I realized how fidgety my companions were. They hung back against the wall, stoically checking their watches. I felt sure they regretted giving me a ride, and I was more than a little relieved when we were permitted to leave.

Tension subsided as the miles between the checkpoint and us grew. My companions resumed their conversation in German. Although I couldn't understand what they said, I knew something was wrong when an announcement on the radio interrupted the music and their conversation suddenly stopped.

"What did the radio say?" I asked. They seemed unable to respond. I repeated my question and waited.

Hans, the driver, switched off the radio and in a flat, tight voice said, "Oswald's been shot."

We all knew that Lee Harvey Oswald was Kennedy's alleged assassin, and a creepy silence followed instead of a postmortem commentary. Listening to the quiet was noise enough for me. I again stared out the window at the trees fading in and out of the slate-gray fog, reflecting the mood in the car. I tried to comprehend what sort of country I came from, questioning the rhetoric about America being a peace-loving nation.

The year before, in 1962, I had completely missed the Cuban Missile Crisis while biking through Ireland. Traveling as I did, I missed a lot of what was happening in the world, which was OK with me. But there was no escaping this current episode. Like the fog, the news of it was everywhere. The shooting of Oswald brought a surreal element to what I was experiencing, and I felt both present and absent.

Gone was the tentative relaxed atmosphere, and the mechanics of watching the clock and checking the mileage resumed until we reached West Berlin. The boys dropped me off at one of the city's three youth hostels. While registering, I was told, "You can stay here tonight, but you'll have to leave tomorrow." The youth hostels in Berlin were popular, and therefore the maximum stay at each was three nights. I moved three times over the next ten days and found the relocating as much an adventure as an inconvenience.

I roamed the city freely, realizing not everyone had that choice. I walked through Checkpoint Charlie or took the train to the Eastern sector, where the wounds of the war from two decades before still festered. Bombed-out buildings and piles of rubble kept the past present. East Berlin contrasted sharply with West Berlin, which had become a vibrant and prosperous metropolis and where the scars of war had faded. Still, Berlin was an island in the middle of East Germany, and feelings of fear and isolation prevailed.

One day, while wandering the streets in East Berlin, I got lost and stopped and asked a girl for directions. When she finally thought she understood me, she kept repeating, "I can't go, I can't go." I tried to explain that I knew she couldn't go but that I could, and I needed her to tell me how to get back to West Berlin. My efforts were futile. Realizing that communication had failed, I left feeling somehow that I was deserting her. When I turned to wave good-bye, there she stood, on a street empty of traffic and people, with a pewter sky and buildings turned to rubble as a backdrop. She appeared distraught, as though it were she who had lost her way.

Being able to travel easily between East and West Berlin made me appreciate the freedom I enjoyed and took for granted as an American. My excursions gave that freedom focus, and although the differences between the Eastern and Western sectors were striking, similarities outweighed those differences. Earlier in the year, while walking across the border between Jordan and Israel, I'd felt I was bridging a time warp spanning two centuries. Unlike the Middle East—where language, culture, and religion separated nations—in Germany, if someone in the Eastern sector wanted coffee, cigarettes, or some other rationed item, a family member or friend from the West was able to send it. There were limitations on how much or how often items could be sent, but the commitment to get supplies to those in the East helped to keep the ties between family and friends from unraveling. With such strong links, it seemed inevitable to me that one day the two sides would again be united.

The day after my arrival in West Berlin, November 25th, Rudolph-Wilde-Platz was renamed John-F.-Kennedy-Platz. In preparation for the dedication, stores closed early. People gathered respectfully in the whispered quiet that filled the square. It was hard to imagine that Kennedy had spoken in the same setting only five months before. The crowds had erupted into jubilation when he identified with them by declaring, "Ich bin ein Berliner."

I stood there, freezing, listening to words I could not understand but could only feel. The packed crowd listened attentively to the speeches, and at the end of the ceremony the speeches were replaced with a somber silence. Nobody left. I, like those around me, remained transfixed. My earlier thoughts of cheering crowds enthusiastically receiving JFK were replaced with images from a darker layer of history. Hitler, from the same platform, had once mesmerized a different cheering crowd.

No one seemed to pay any attention to the announcements over the loudspeakers asking the assemblage to leave. Perhaps it was the weight of history that made leaving so difficult, or possibly psychological inertia. It was only after the police started pushing people along that the crowd finally dispersed. I fell into step with the one-way pedestrian traffic that flowed quietly down streets already dressed for Christmas.

After a week, having used up my time limits at the youth hostels, I moved to the Bahnhof Mission, a homeless shelter located in the train station. I'd slept under trucks and in toilet stalls during the previous months and therefore found my mission lodging quite acceptable. It was musty, cold, and damp but within my budget.

I left Berlin on December 1st. It took me four hours to make my way from the center of the city through its outskirts to the autobahn. It shouldn't have. I had gotten lost and ended up taking the same bus to the same end point twice. The population thinned out, and I found myself virtually alone by the time I reached the autobahn corridor that would take me to the checkpoint.

The energy was eerie, but I just kept on walking, trying to ignore the unfamiliar feelings of apprehension. I knew that once I reached the checkpoint I would be able to get a ride all the way to Hanover. Because there were no other hitchhikers around, I tried to reassure myself that getting a ride would be easier.

I often found myself totally disconnected from the rest of the world, which generally suited me just fine, but on this occasion it felt unsettling. In a thoughtful mood, I became preoccupied in looking for treasures that might have flown out of car windows. My pack weighed over thirty-five pounds, so I was selective about what I kept. Because it was cold, I decided when I discovered a beautiful wool scarf on the shoulder of the road that it was a keeper and wrapped it around my head and mouth. I couldn't believe its owner hadn't returned for it.

Looking up to see how much farther the checkpoint was, I saw soldiers in a lookout tower camouflaged by trees. I smiled and waved. They waved back. It was reassuring to see a couple of human beings. But after walking another five or ten minutes, two soldiers popped out of the thicket of trees. Each grabbed one of my arms and forcefully escorted me up the wooded incline and through three layers of barbed-wire fencing. I was more surprised than scared. I didn't try to resist them but kept asking, "Are you East or West? Are you East or West?"

One finally comprehended and said, "East, East, no West here." I was so pleased to have communicated that the fact they were East Germans seemed secondary. The thicket of trees running parallel to the road had provided ample cover for them, and because I had been so preoccupied with my treasure hunt, they had never even entered my field of vision.

They kept repeating, "fünf Minuten, fünf Minuten" ("five minutes"), which soon gave way to "dreissig Minuten, dreissig Minuten" ("thirty minutes"). My response, "Ja ja dreissig jahr" (thirty years), and this time it was they who appeared pleased that communication had taken place. They laughed nervously as they shook their heads, indicating it would not be that long. They appeared ill at ease, which I somehow found reassuring.

The two of them ushered me through the trees to an opening where an army truck and another four soldiers waited. One of them motioned for me to get into the back of a truck. "Maybe that won't be necessary," I said, as though I was the one in charge. I continued to chat away as I rummaged through my rucksack, found and showed them my passport with confidence. They patiently watched my performance and then helped me into the back of the truck.

The truck made the only noise as we bumped along through cold, damp fog. When we arrived at a compound, about a dozen soldiers were outside their barracks, as if waiting for my arrival. Some shouted, "Hi." I felt conspicuous as one of the soldiers led and another followed me upstairs to a sparsely furnished room, where the commander in charge sat behind a large wooden desk. Sitting across from him, I restarted my chatter, this time with less confidence. I again produced my passport, and again it was not my passport to freedom. He watched me with focused attention, waiting for me to realize that I was not going anywhere.

They spoke among themselves in German. I could understand a word here and there but never enough to provide meaning to the discussions taking place. Periodically there was a nod in my direction, and at one point one of the soldiers asked through a motion of his hand if I'd like to rest on the cot in the corner. I declined but thought it a good sign that they were interested in my welfare.

When the commander left, communication with my guard took the form of charades. I dug through my rucksack and found a well-used deck of playing cards. I taught him how to play gin rummy and prided myself on being able to count to ten in German. When we tired of this, I poked around in my rucksack again, this time producing a kit for blowing up plastic balloons. The last time I had made any balloons was in Egypt, where young children had gathered around me to watch.

First I put a glob of plastic on the end of a plastic straw, blew it up, and then pinched it off. The sticky balloons dried quickly, and my guard and I drew faces on them. The inappropriateness of the activity was brought home when the commander returned to find us playing with balloons. He was clearly not pleased and dismissed the befuddled guard, who retreated, gave a perfunctory salute, and almost stumbled as he backed out through the door.

Once the commander and I were alone, his voice toned down, and he asked me to sing American songs. I thought this rivaled what he had just criticized moments before and pointed to the radio. He shook his head, indicating they were forbidden to tune in Western stations. So for my command performance I sang a somewhat shaky "Zip-a-Dee-Doo-Dah." No other song came to mind, and I felt fortunate that he could not understand the words. He seemed unimpressed with my performance.

The concert was interrupted by food: pork, red cabbage, and potatoes. Cabbage never smelled so good; the meal was the best I'd had in a long time. My captors apologized for not offering coffee. The soldier who brought the food was directed to give me a cigarette. His moment of reluctance and pained expression told me they were rationed, and the gesture itself reassured me again of their interest in making me comfortable.

I don't think I craved the cigarette as much as the soldier who parted with it, but I took it anyway and thanked him. With the commander and a couple of soldiers in the room at the same time, the games and singing stopped. Unaware at the time that we were waiting for an interpreter, whose job it would be to interrogate me, I retreated into my own thoughts. I realized how very much alone I was. I became acutely aware that for the first time in my life, I was experiencing what many others constantly lived with: the knowledge that I was not a free person.

Although appropriately apprehensive, I wasn't scared. Witnessing myself as though I were in a play, I clearly sensed the soldiers had no interest in harming me. Having left center stage, I sat and watched the daylight in the small window behind the desk fade to black.

When the interpreter arrived, I presented him with what I no longer thought of as my passport to freedom. He examined it with great interest, pulling out the extensions that had been added to accommodate additional visas and country entry and exit stamps. It was then that I asked, "Why did they pick me up?"

He hadn't responded to my naive reply about the American flag, but I felt he knew I was American. Given his response that I was the first American they had picked up, coupled with JFK's recent assassination, I suddenly realized they weren't quite sure what to do with me.

"Do you know anyone in the military?" he asked. I said I didn't, but that was not true. I saw no advantage in admitting that I had recently stayed with a college classmate in Verdun, France, whose father happened to be the commanding general for the American troops based there.

"No one in the world who knows me has any idea where I am." That was true. "This is my last stop. My plan is to go back to the States when I leave here." I moved quickly to change the subject. "What are the East German people being told was the reason for Kennedy's assassination?"

The interpreter did not hesitate: "It's because he signed the nuclear test-ban treaty." I went over and pawed though my rucksack, locating the newspapers and magazines I had collected in Munich and Berlin and gave them to him. He flipped through the pages of *Time* and pointed to a picture showing Ruby shooting Oswald. "What do you think of that? He has a phone in his cell and can walk around and hold meetings." He hadn't had time to read what the caption said, so I assumed his information came from another source. If true, he clearly was more informed than I.

A soldier entered the room and interrupted our conversation. German replaced English, and after a brief exchange I learned that they planned to take me back to Berlin. Knowing how hard it would be to find a place to stay, I asked, "Can't you just take me to the checkpoint? It's taken me all day to get this far." The directness of my request surprised them, but they agreed to see what they could do. Numerous phone calls were made, and the earlier patience exhibited toward me melted away. As the novelty of my presence decreased, the gruffness of their voices increased. Reading the dialogue with mounting anxiety, I was relieved when it was finally announced that my request had been approved and we would leave immediately.

As I was helped into the back of the truck, I noted my entourage now included a German shepherd, which was providing plenty of exercise for the soldier at the end of its leash. The commander sat in the cab with the driver. Even though it was dark, I knew we were not returning to the same place where I'd been picked up. The road became narrower and muddier. Looking out through the flapping canvas at the back of the truck, I kept thinking, "curtains for Keekee, curtains for Keekee," and for the first time I thought with a sinking feeling that the drama might not have a happy ending.

Suddenly we stopped. The commander came to the back of the truck and motioned for me to get out. I missed the English-speaking official. "No," I said. If I was going to be shot, I was not going to walk willingly to that destination.

The commander motioned for me to look to the other side of the truck, where the lights of the checkpoint could be seen in the distance. He pointed to the headlights, indicating that we would be spotted if we went further. Realizing I had no choice, I got out. One of the soldiers carried my rucksack, another worked at restraining the German shepherd, and a third directed me with his gun to walk with the commander.

No one said anything. Frozen leaves crunched under our feet as we approached the barbed wire. Feeling uneasy with the gun pointed at my back, I inadvertently moved to the right. The soldiers instinctively shouted; fear stiffened me. I was grabbed and pulled back into formation. Although at the time the thought never registered, in retrospect it seems probable that the area was mined. Quiet returned, except for the crunching sound.

When we reached the barbed wire, I knew I was closer to the checkpoint than I had been in the morning; four rather than three layers of barbed wire separated us from the autobahn. The soldier who had carried my pack helped me on with it, and in good German fashion I shook hands with the commander. The gesture seemed as appropriate as it did inappropriate.

My pack lurched heavily from side to side as I lumbered toward the lights in the distance. Although my departure had been civil enough, I half expected to be shot. As I neared the perimeter of light, a West German border guard came toward me and asked if I had tried crossing in the morning. Relieved, I responded, "As a matter of fact, yes."

Motioning me to follow him, he said, "How do you feel after being detained in Russian territory for over four hours?" As he led me to a makeshift conference room, he continued, "Someone saw you being taken this morning. We've been on the lookout for you."

I met with American and West German military personnel. I expected those assembled around the table to be friendly and welcoming, but the debriefing did not have the conversational tone I had experienced in the East. Their barrage of questions surprised me:

"Who was in charge—East Germans or the Russians?"

"What color were their uniforms, brown or gray? What rank was the commander?"

"What was rationed? How many soldiers are stationed there?"

"Did they harm you in any way?"

"What kind of questions did they ask you?"

They finally ran out of questions. The only piece of information that seemed new to them was the second break in the barbed wire that separated East Germany from the autobahn that stretched through it.

I was told that because they had detained me for over an hour, the East Germans would know. If I chose to go on, they would take no responsibility for me. They meant it. Their argument was persuasive. A military patrol was dispatched to take me back to the American sector, and I was instructed that I was to meet with the American consul at 9 a.m. the following morning. All the attention made me feel both important and a nuisance.

The American GIs were more than a little surprised when I asked them to deposit me at the Bahnhof mission. The surly registrar was irritated when she saw me enter: "Why did you say you were leaving this morning if you were coming back tonight?" Too tired to explain, I simply apologized. Begrudgingly, she assigned me a cot. Exhausted, I fell asleep immediately.

For my official meeting the next day, I wore pants I'd been issued when working on the kibbutz in Israel and a well-worn shirt. I felt about as charming as I looked when I reported for my meeting with the consul promptly at nine. Neither of us was particularly interested in seeing the other, but both of us were interested in getting me out of Berlin. Since rail and road were not options because they went through East Germany, we agreed I'd fly. After going over a condensed version of the previous day's events, we looked over the flight schedule. He then called for a car, and I was whisked off to the airport, where I boarded the next plane to Hanover.

The world was thrown off balance with the assassination of Kennedy. Time and experience have helped me realize how fortunate I was not to have been shot. I have always felt that Kennedy's assassination, in some indirect way, played a part in restraining those who could have done me harm.

Generations have experienced collective moments in history when the American psyche has resonated as one: the bombing of Pearl Harbor, the assassination of JFK, and the 9/11 terrorist attacks. More than a half-century has passed since the Berlin Wall was built and more than a quarter of a century since it came down. The memory of my particular experience is reprinted in my mind every November, and with each printing the focus sharpens on how our lives become history.

Part II

Peace Corps India
1965–67

APPLYING TO THE PEACE CORPS

View of the maidan *from my chawl in Worli (Bombay)*

At the end of 1963 I returned to the States and applied to the Peace Corps immediately. Knowing it would take a while, I kept myself occupied by teaching third grade in Ohio for three months. I quickly realized that some of the third graders could read better than I could, and most could spell better. (At the time I didn't know I was dyslexic.) I solved the spelling problem by rewarding Pam, who always spelled everything correctly, with the privilege of grading all the spelling tests except hers. She was honored by the recognition and carried out the task willingly. For reading class, I brought in a very bulky tape recorder so the students could hear how they read. We had a good time.

Although the principal wanted lesson plans at the beginning of each week, I explained that wasn't possible for my class as we voted each morning on how to organize our day. Even though I didn't follow the prescribed way of doing things, the administration thought I was a fabulous teacher. I knew my real skill lay in creating alternatives on how to get around traditional ways of teaching.

In the spring I received a call from the Peace Corps asking whether I would like to join a training group destined for Liberia. In my own mind I had been thinking of India, for no better reason than it was far away and sounded exotic. Not knowing I had a choice, I accepted and set off in June for training at San Francisco State College. The group, Liberia IV, was the largest training group thus far. My assignment, after I completed training satisfactorily, would be to teach in an elementary school. Of the 200 trainees, 90 were expected to replace some of the 235 Peace Corps volunteers currently serving as teachers in Liberia; the others would be placed in new teaching situations.

Midway through training, three people in the group were deselected (a Peace Corps euphemism for firing potential volunteers). One was a woman in her 70s and in poor health, another was a fellow who made it clear that his primary interest was to convert all of Africa to Christianity, and the third was ME!

I was shocked, as I thought I was perfect for the Peace Corps. Thinking it must be a mistake, I marched off to the Peace Corps office, where they assured me it wasn't a mistake. I was informed that those in power thought I would not be a good fit. I was frustrated and pointed out that I had come back from my travels specifically to join the Peace Corps. When I insisted that I deserved a better answer, I was finally told, "We think you're too independent."

I was dumbfounded and just sat there, as the woman giving me the verdict babbled on, "If you go get a job and stay in one place for a year or so, you can always reapply." She ended with, "You don't need to worry. We'll pay for your plane ticket back home."

"And where would that be?" I asked. I didn't have a Plan B. Knowing I could not argue with the "too independent" label, I proceeded to successfully negotiate for money in lieu of a plane ticket. The request was granted on the condition that I leave immediately.

The next day I left for Albuquerque to visit Carla, my sophomore roommate from college. On the bus I had plenty of time to think about my rejection. I'd been quite open about my unorthodox and somewhat chancy way of traveling during the preceding year, and I assumed the Peace Corps considered me too much of a risk. They probably thought I would go to Liberia, work for a few months, get bored, and decide to hitchhike across North Africa, possibly convincing a few other volunteers to join me. They might have been right about my becoming bored, but I think they would have been wrong about my quitting.

From Albuquerque I continued by bus to New York City, where I got a job with the Bureau of Child Welfare. I interviewed prospective foster parents for infants who had been abandoned in hospitals. After working there for about a year, I was again accepted by the Peace Corps, this time to train with a group slated for Bombay, India. I realized then that my deselection from the Liberian group had been a blessing and a lesson. It taught me that if something doesn't work out, life will often present a better option. India was where I'd wanted to go in the first place.

Our training took place at the Columbia University School of Social Work in New York City. I lived in East Harlem because the Peace Corps higher-ups thought there might be a parallel between poverty in Harlem and poverty in the slums of Bombay. Once in India, many of us laughed about this unrealistic comparison. Our group, India XXIII, was trained in urban community development (UCD). The program emulated Saul Alinsky's approach of motivating members of communities to collectively come together and become directly involved in making changes to improve their lives. It was a pilot project, the first of its kind to be undertaken by the Peace Corps in Asia, and considered high-risk, high-gain.

Of the fifty-eight who began training, forty-four— including three of us deselected from other training groups—became volunteers. Most were middle-class college graduates whose reasons for joining the Peace Corps varied. A few of the guys were not interested in going to Vietnam to fight a war; other trainees were at a loss about what to do after graduating. I wanted to continue to travel and see the world. Underlying all of these reasons was the impact of Kennedy's speech: "Ask not what your country can do for you, ask what you can do for your country."

Our group, packed with energy, enthusiasm, and commitment, departed for India in January of 1966. We arrived in Bombay shortly before dawn. Most airports did not allow planes to come and go during the wee hours of the morning, and Bombay appeared to have cornered that niche market. When we disembarked, there were people everywhere: women in colorful saris, men in Nehru dress, all shouting and waving to get the attention of deplaning passengers. It was clearly a social event, but it was hard to comprehend that all this activity was taking place in what felt like the middle of the night.

Luggage was pushed on unmechanized rollers. Coolies (manual laborers) bullied their way through the crowd and snatched up suitcases. Owners waved at them from across the terminal, pointing in the direction where suitcases and owners could connect. Our group was somewhat protected from all the chaos. Peace Corps staff whisked us off to a waiting bus, while others took charge of our luggage. We left the cacophony of activity as dawn broke and made our way from the outskirts of the city to a two-star hotel in downtown Bombay. There we would spend the next couple of days getting oriented and receiving our assignments.

The ride into the city reminded me of a movie trailer, previewing what we would be experiencing during our two-year assignments. Although it was still very early, some pavement dwellers were already rolling up their sleeping mats. Cows (the most revered animals in India) and goats wandered in the street and they served to reorganize traffic patterns more effectively than any policeman could. The sultry air was saturated with the smell of diesel fuel and garbage, and the sounds of the city waking up became louder as we neared the hotel. Clearly India was going to stimulate and exhaust my senses.

As I walked around Bombay, India began to sink in. It was during those first few days of seeing throngs of people everywhere that I decided my life's work would be in the field of population and family planning. Therefore it almost seemed prophetic that my assigned housing ended up being in a maternity hospital.

SETTLING INTO WORLI CHAWLS

Savantha, Keekee, and Kishore beside 50 BDD
Chawl (Worli Maternity Hospital)

The Peace Corps placed Melody, another volunteer, and me in the Worli chawls, a Bombay community of 60,000 located near the Arabian Sea. We moved into the one designated as the maternity hospital for the area. The chawls were built by the British in the early 1900s to house mill workers. Each of the 121 cement buildings had four floors, twenty rooms on a floor, and footprint toilets at the end of each hallway—fortunately not at our end. The rooms measured ten by fourteen feet, and in the corner, cement blocks partitioned off a four-foot-square area where we bathed by scooping water from buckets. We left the spigot open so that our hour of rationed water, which began spurting at 5:30 each morning, could serve as an alarm clock.

Within a few days, Melody and I converted what many would think of as a cell into a home. We had little furniture—two narrow beds housed under mosquito netting. We hung our clothes on hooks cemented into the wall and draped colorful material over the barred windows; the bars made me feel protected rather than trapped. We purchased two buckets (to collect water), a fan, and a kerosene stove. In the weeks to come, Melody and I would add an old English rocker for $15 and a small table. After each addition, I would declare the room near perfection.

Although we found our room small, the average number living in duplicate floor-plans throughout the community was seven. Kerosene stoves in each room hinted at the number of households living there. The most I found claiming to live in one room was thirty-nine. People flowed in from the villages more easily than water. At night many of the men slept on the *maidan*, a centrally located sun-baked dusty area about the size of a football field. Dr. Dharap, the head of the hospital, approached Melody and me about using our room during the day as a day care center. We knew space was at a premium but said no, as we needed some semblance of privacy.

Cultural exchange was one of the Peace Corps' goals, and because cell phones and the Internet had yet to be invented, this goal received more emphasis and had greater impact in the early days of the program. By living in the community, I was able to bring the outside world to my neighbors with unplanned nuggets of information. For example, I showed Savantha, a woman living a few buildings away, a photo of the house where I grew up. I knew from her expression that the photo, taken after a major snowstorm, confused her. She looked at it curiously and wanted to know why the house and bushes had so many layers of whitewash. I explained that in really cold weather, rain becomes snow, the white stuff. Because temperatures in Bombay never got below freezing, she had no experiential framework in which to put such a fact. She remained mystified.

A week later I interviewed Savantha to be our cook. Because tuberculosis was prevalent and most people suffered from various kinds of dysentery, the Peace Corps required that cooks have physicals. Savantha had never been more than two miles from Worli and was more nervous than excited when I took her for her exam. After she was treated with antibiotics for dysentery, we employed her for the equivalent of $3 a month.

Most cooks worked full time. Refrigeration was rare, and therefore cooks went to the market every day before spending hours preparing labor-intensive, and delicious, meals. Because Melody and I did the shopping and Savantha's cooking skills were extremely limited, her salary of $3 was fair. Of greater value, for which there was no price tag, was the status she gained in the community.

Savantha was a Buddhist, as were most in her chawl. As an untouchable (*Dalit*) in India, she was stuck at the bottom of the Hindu caste system, with no chance of changing her status in this lifetime. Understandably, Savantha and tens of thousands of untouchables like her chose to convert to Buddhism or Christianity. Hindus continued to see her as an untouchable, but she saw herself differently, as a human being having value.

Many were surprised and perplexed when we employed Savantha to be our cook. Traditionally, those in higher castes prepare food for those in lower castes. (Brahmins, the highest caste, are often cooks.) Some excused our perceived ignorance because we were foreigners. Others, because they weren't quite sure where we fit in the caste system, chose not to express an opinion. Still others were pleased. Hearing about Savantha's good fortune gave many Dalits hope that maybe their own status could be changed during their lifetime.

Savantha came every day and cooked rice and *dhal* (stewed lentils) over a kerosene stove in our room. The menu was monotonous, so one day I decided to go to a nearby Muslim community and buy meat. Flies attacked me as I entered the butcher shop, and the stench of rotting meat was a clear sign that I should turn around and leave, but I didn't. I decided to make a purchase primarily because I didn't want to disappoint the two enthusiastic butchers who laughingly fell over each other to serve me. They warned me that my selection was dog meat, but I thought they were kidding. Regardless, my thinking was that cooking would kill whatever might be wrong with the meat.

Savantha was not happy about cooking the meat, which was stringy and putrid. Dr. Dharap was even more distressed. She said the patients were complaining that the smell was making them sick and told me that in the future, all meat was to be cooked on the roof. The request was not really necessary, as Melody and I got sick too. The experience convinced me to become a vegetarian while in India.

Learning about the community was essential. In visiting various chawls, I occasionally stumbled onto someone who spoke a little English. The Peace Corps taught us Hindi, which had just been declared the national language, but the language in the state of Maharashtra, where Bombay is located, was Marathi, and those I met who knew Hindi generally knew English. Because multiple dialects and languages were spoken throughout India, the selection of Hindi angered many people. Thousands went on strike and demonstrated in the streets. By default, and over time, English became the bridge between and among the various Indian languages.

While assessing the few services provided in the Worli community, I came across the People's Mobile Hospital. There I met Kishor, a most unusual man, who became a close and loyal friend during my two years in Bombay. He had flown for the Japanese during World War II but made it clear he would have been happy to fly for the Americans—he just liked to fly. He was shorter than my 5'2" frame and claimed that his loss of height was due to spending four years in an army prison camp during the war.

His job at the hospital, which was under construction, seemed to be one of making sure that the workers actually worked. After we had tea, he rattled off instructions to various workers and then insisted we go for a ride in his Jeep. I didn't have any idea where he wanted to go but intuitively trusted him. We stopped at a Catholic church, a Buddhist temple, and a Hindu temple. He said he believed in "keeping his bases covered."

Before dropping me off, he announced that I needed to meet the Ruparels, the family primarily involved with the construction of the hospital. He said he'd make arrangements for us to have dinner with them the following week and would arrange to pick me up. It was a command, not an invitation.

The next week Kishor collected me from the maternity hospital, and off we went to meet the Ruparels. On the way he told me what a generous family they were and that they had given him the Jeep. When we arrived at their residence, a spacious bungalow on Malabar Hill, it was immediately apparent that Kishor, who I later learned was orphaned as a child, was treated as a member of the family.

The Ruparels were industrialists who had originally come to Bombay from Kutch, a district in Gujarat. The extended family included two brothers, their wives, and an unmarried sister, Manik. The only offspring, Shrikant, was at Oxford in England. They were a charitable family and involved in a number of philanthropic endeavors, including Ruparel College and a temple in downtown Bombay, as well as the Ruparel Medical Centre (People's Mobile Hospital) in Worli.

Although the hospital wasn't finished, the mobile vans, which traveled to the suburbs to provide medical services, were operational. I would sometimes accompany one of the medical teams on their scheduled visits: two locations in the morning and two in the afternoon. Invariably, a line of patients would be waiting.

It was incomprehensible to the Ruparels that a young American would come to live and work in the slums of Bombay. Every month or so, either the family would send a car or Kishor would pick me up for an elaborate event or a meal at the Ruparel home. Like Kishor, I became a part of the family and was included in many celebrations— birthdays, national holidays, weddings, and so on. With Shrikant away in England, I came to think of myself as his generational replacement.

Because all members of the family spoke English and made an effort to teach me about their culture, customs, and religion, I always felt comfortable in asking them questions. On occasion, the cook, who was a Brahmin, would serve. He always hesitated when he came to me. When I asked Manik why, she explained that he was afraid I might touch him. If I did, he would throw out the food he was serving, go take a bath, put on clean clothes, and perform *puja* (an act of worship) to cleanse his soul before he resumed his duties. Clearly he must have seen me as an untouchable.

The cook was one of the twenty-four servants employed by the Ruparels. In addition to those who worked in buying, preparing, and serving food, there were four drivers, round-the-clock watchmen, sweepers, gardeners, and *dhobis,* who laundered clothes. Additionally, a live-in priest performed puja each morning before the large sterling-silver altar. It was located in a room on the ground floor, adjacent to the central gathering area. Before each meal, he would place offerings, samples of the food to be served, in front of the altar and bless them.

It was a religious household, and during my years as a Peace Corps volunteer, liquor was never served in the Ruparel home. Narandas, the younger brother, did imbibe outside the home. One time Kishor, Narandas, another Peace Corps volunteer and I went to the Harbour Bar in the Taj Hotel for a drink. There were not that many places you could go for a drink, and during those years, in order to be served, one needed a liquor permit. In the application for mine, I'd put "national custom." You surrendered your permit when you entered an establishment and regained possession of it when you left. The amount of liquor consumed by an individual would be noted in his or her permit.

On this particular occasion, the waiter came over and asked me to identify myself. He returned a few minutes later and handed me my permit: "Please sign here, *memsahib*." In it was written, "I was not in need of liquors during April 1967 and May 1967 and hence no purchases were made during these months." I signed it. Although the system for obtaining and consuming liquor was closely monitored, there were ways of getting around the restrictions for those who had money and connections.

Regardless of economic status, tea was generally offered. Sometimes when I visited a chawl, a runner was sent to the store to buy me a Coke. I would try to refuse, as I knew it was an extravagance they would not treat themselves to. They would insist, and I understood early on that it was an argument I would not win. I tried to rectify the situation by taking a few sips of the Coke and then giving the bottle to one of the children gazing up at me from the floor or hovering in the doorway.

Frequently there would also be food. No matter what I ate at the Ruparels, I knew for certain I wouldn't get sick. When I accepted food given to me in the chawls, I was just as sure I probably would. Because I knew they would be insulted if I didn't accept food offered, I often took the risk and paid the price. I finally solved the problem by telling people it was a fast day for me. This excuse was always accepted and respected.

Although people loved it when I visited them in the chawls, I wasn't successful in helping them to improve their lives. The community center located across the maidan from the hospital was underutilized. I put together a small library of books collected primarily from the United States Information Service (USIS). I don't think many of the books were ever read. I arranged for a nutritionist to come to the center and give a lecture on wholesome foods—again, an effort I consider a failure, because few in the area could afford to buy many of the foods suggested. I arranged for Dr. Dada Pai, a local physician, to talk about family planning, another—failure. His suggestions for using contraception to provide space between pregnancies for the health of both mother and child were ignored. Some of the women told me that it was their moral obligation to have children. How else could unborn souls advance through karma to higher states?

Dr. Pai was passionate about family planning and became known internationally for his efforts in this area. He introduced the red triangle as an icon for family planning. A decade later, when I was working for the Planned Parenthood Federation of American in its international division, I would always think of him whenever I saw one of these triangles, which by then were all over Africa and other parts of Asia.

I appreciated Dr. Pai's passion but understood the predicament faced by those in India. Children there, as well as those in other developing countries, served as a social security system. Having many children increased the odds that a couple of them would survive to take care of their aging parents. Although I could not comprehend how India could manage to feed any more people, the green revolution was beginning to have an impact. Technology was increasing agriculture production worldwide. The population of India grew rapidly, and has doubled in size since I lived there as a volunteer.

Although I felt strongly about family planning, my assignment was in urban community development. As time passed, many of the volunteers moved into more structured and, in many cases, more satisfying assignments. Although I could not point to one success, I and a few others were not ready to give up on the Peace Corps' pilot UCD program in Asia. We continued to flounder in our nebulous assignments but also started discussing among ourselves the idea of implementing a community development project in another setting.

I felt guilty taking up space in the maternity hospital and realized early on that many of the nurses were confused by my presence and unclear as to why I was there. I was flabbergasted when one of them asked me if I would like to examine a patient who was about to deliver. My instinctive response to laugh was replaced with a smile. I explained that although my father was a surgeon, I had no medical training. Their asking me to examine a patient made me wonder how clear the communication had been between the Peace Corps and hospital staff.

The miscommunication prompted me to ask Dr. Dharap if I could observe a delivery. I'd never seen one of these everyday miracles, and because I was living in a maternity hospital, it seemed like a perfect opportunity. I could not imagine such a synchronistic situation presenting itself back in the States, and the likelihood that such a request would be granted was even more unimaginable. Decades later, with the introduction of the Health Insurance Portability and Accountability Act (HIPAA), and its emphasis on privacy, agreeing to such a request would be inconceivable. But this was India. Dr. Dharap seemed pleased that I was interested in observing a delivery and said she would arrange it.

As a Peace Corps volunteer, there were numerous occasions when I received special treatment. Often, in the early days of the program, volunteers found themselves in communities where many of its members had never met a foreigner. Fortunately, or unfortunately, time and technology has made the world much more interconnected, and volunteers today are less likely to be seen or treated as special as they were back then.

Cultural exchanges were sometimes subtle, sometimes structured. In all cases, they were learning experiences for me and for those I interacted with. I felt the exchange rate was always in my favor. I know those in my Peace Corps group strongly agree that we gained much more than we ever gave, and the experiences we had while living in India have impacted our lives in ways that continue to this day.

An Indian Birth

As Dr. Dharap accompanied me to the delivery room, I bombarded her with questions. I felt like a reporter getting a backstory. Knowing there was a strong preference for boys in India, I asked, "Have you ever had a problem with a woman claiming she gave birth to a boy instead of a girl?"

"Oh no," she insisted. "That's never been a problem in the thirty-four years the hospital's been here. We have a policy that as soon as a woman delivers, we hold up the newborn and have the mother say out loud whether it's a boy or a girl." She answered other questions: "We average six deliveries a day.... Some women come here from the villages to deliver.... We have thirty-four beds.... The women receive two meals a day." She continued, "Most are not interested in family planning, but if a woman accepts an IUD, she will get five rupees (thirty-seven cents) and the hospital will get two. The problem is that many of them have an IUD inserted just for the money, and a week or so later they will go to another clinic and have it removed. We do not encourage the pill. The women cannot remember to take one every day, the rats eat them, and sometimes the husbands take them, thinking that will prevent pregnancies. Education is too difficult."

The doctor left after introducing me to the two nurses in charge of the day's deliveries. The delivery room was clean but looked shabby with its cement floors and walls of peeling blue paint. Two women were already lying on parallel tables covered with previously stained plastic sheets.

The first birth, a girl, was held up and identified by the mother, who seemed visibly disappointed. One of the nurses helped the mother off the table and supported her as she walked to the recovery room. The nurse returned a few minutes later with another woman in labor. She was rewarded with the birth of a boy, whose sex was identified with joy. Praise and congratulations erupted spontaneously. A healthy son.... The gods had been good to her. When the nurse left the room with her and the newborn, the joy and bliss of the moment left with them.

In the heavy energy left behind, the focus of attention turned toward the woman on the other table. She had been all but ignored, and the anguish on her face spoke more loudly than her muffled groans. One nurse explained, "She is from village, very sick, very anemic, has high fever, 104 degrees. She must deliver today or maybe she die." The woman in labor choked out whispered pleas in a dialect neither of the nurses seemed to understand. They addressed this problem by speaking loudly, punctuating the local language of Marathi with English for my benefit.

I winced as I witnessed them slapping the woman and poking her with scissors, demanding that she push harder and reprimanding her for not doing her part. It was difficult to watch. I wondered whether my presence influenced the nurses' behavior in any way. Surely one nurse torturing the poor woman was enough. And why didn't one of them go for the doctor? I said nothing. As an invited observer I thought interjecting my opinion might be interpreted as meddling, which it would be. There was already enough tension in the room.

Feeling uncomfortable and useless, I went over to the window, pulled aside the plastic curtains, and peeked through the iron bars. Next to the road, a cow rested in the shade of the bus stand, leaving the people waiting for the bus to bake in the sun. Below, I watched children playing in the dust, their shouts of laughter drowning out the groans of the woman in labor.

The moaning finally stopped, but no crying replaced it. I turned and saw that the newborn was blue. During the moments of confusion that followed, the nurses failed to hold up the newborn, a girl, for identification. Instead, they put her on a side table and scurried off to get oxygen and, hopefully, the doctor. Although I received no instructions, I felt as though I'd been left in charge.

The new mother turned and faced the wall. Her long black hair was plastered to her head with perspiration, and her frail, exhausted body lay limp under a thin, frayed blanket. I tiptoed around the table to see whether her eyes were open. They were but stared blankly. I could only imagine what she was thinking, feeling, if anything.

The room had become quite still; the only noise was borrowed from outside. Temptation led me over to the table, where I unfolded the wrinkled miniature hand to look at the lifeline: it was long. When the nurses returned with oxygen a few minutes later, I moved away from the table so they could work on the newborn.

As I observed what was happening, I was also witnessing myself. What was I doing there? It was as though I was an understudy for a part I hadn't read. I was good at taking in information, noting all that was going on around me, but what did the part call for? The room was charged with tension and emotion as the two nurses tried frantically to save the baby. I wanted very much to stay and see the experience through to the end but felt my presence awkward and so excused myself. "I'm leaving now. I'm going upstairs to my room." Thanking them did not seem appropriate.

I realized how hot it was as I climbed the steep cement steps with effort. Thoughts of snow falling in New York months before had long ago melted into memory. The temperature fluctuated between hot and hotter. I entered the room and collapsed on my bed, thankful that Melody and I had not agreed to have our room used as a nursery during the day. Staring up at the mosquito net draped over the frame of my bed, I couldn't help thinking about what was happening downstairs. I wished I'd stayed, even though leaving was the right thing to do.

The following morning, as I went downstairs to inquire about how the mother and newborn were doing, I met one of the nurses who had been in attendance the day before. She spoke with concern: "The baby died at 2 last night. Mother saying the child is not hers. She saying she had boy. Word sent to father in village. Maybe he accept baby."

I needed closure and was curious about what they had done with the newborn. "May I see the baby?" The nurse's eyebrows jumped a bit. After a moment of hesitation, she turned and led me to the storage room, where she took down a metal box from a cluttered shelf. It looked like the laundry box I had used in boarding school. She placed it on a table, untied the cord, and removed the top. There was the lifeless newborn, wrapped in swaddling clothes. A blue inked identifying number was clearly marked across its forehead. So much for the long lifeline.

I left the hospital pondering why, after the tens of thousands of births that had taken place there, I was present for that particular one. I thought I would have time to reflect on this, but the presence of so much life and activity in my neighborhood pushed the experience from my mind.

Across the street on the maidan, a few remaining men who had taken shelter under the stars instead of in overcrowded rooms were rolling up their sleeping mats. A long queue waited for buses that might or might not come. Vendors squatted on the edges of sidewalks, selling small stacks of dusty chilies, onions, potatoes, and beans arranged neatly on pieces of cloth. The entrepreneur with the largest inventory was a man hawking a wide selection of empty used bottles. They didn't look clean to me, but obviously there was a market for them.

When I returned to the maternity hospital in the afternoon, I was informed that two policemen were there to see me. As the nurse in the morning had told me, the mother of the unclaimed newborn was claiming she had given birth to a son, not a daughter. I was told the Worli police had arranged to have the body taken to the J. J. Hospital morgue. It was still unclear who would take responsibility for it.

I went to the small room where the two policemen were having tea while they waited for my arrival. They seemed to think I was the only credible witness to the deliveries that had taken place the day before, and that those more directly involved might have some reason to lie about the sex of the third birth. I concurred with the hospital staff's account. "Yes, the first delivery was a girl; the second, a boy; and the third, a girl.... Yes, I would be willing to talk to the mother if that would help."

One of the policemen, the two nurses, and I went to the room where the mother sat on the floor completely shrouded by a worn gray blanket. I did not talk to her. Instead, the nurses talked to her, in Marathi and English, explaining that there was no reason for me to lie. I am sure the poor woman did not understand anything that was said, and soon realized that my presence was not to help console her but rather to corroborate the nurses' story. Their version of what happened was true, but they appeared to be more concerned about their own credibility than about the poor woman who sat silently at my feet. I was no longer an observer; I was now part of the story.

When I returned to the hospital a few days later, one of the nurses came running out to meet me; others gathered on the cement steps at the side entrance of the building. Another rushed up with a newspaper and proudly pointed out my name. I was suddenly a celebrity, credited with bringing closure to a dispute over the death of a newborn girl. The father had agreed to accept the dead newborn as his, and arrangements had been made for her cremation.

As a result of the incident, I received undeserved credit for helping to preserve the reputation of the hospital. The hospital did not get its day nursery, but for some of the staff, my unexpected contribution in upholding its reputation was more valuable. For them, my being there at that moment of time was no accident; karma had dictated that it be so.

BOMBAY HEAT

Shellacked with perspiration, Bombay's population of five million wilted while waiting for the monsoon rains. The monsoon was late, and long, straggly lines of parched people waited for hours to collect a few inches of rationed water from community sources. The water looked like weak tea and served as a halfway house for bacteria in search of a new host. In some parts of the city, the water had ceased to come at all.

Rumors flowed much more freely, and daily I heard of yet another factory closing. The day the Coca-Cola plant closed, I knew things were really serious. There was talk of evacuating hundreds of thousands of people from the city, but to where? Just the thought of the layered Indian bureaucracy undertaking such a project struck me as both funny and sad.

Sensible people were doing as little as possible. Although I planned to go to Crawford Market to buy food for the day, I was restless and decided I would try to locate the Johnsons, a Peace Corps couple in my group. The gossip circulating among volunteers was that they had moved into a newly constructed air-conditioned apartment on the top floor of a welfare center. Not only would it be fun to see them, but I also wanted to check out the air-conditioning rumor.

There was a ten-year waiting list for a telephone, and because numbers dialed were often quite different from numbers reached, I knew it would be an exercise in futility to try to call the welfare center in advance. The directions I had for the Johnsons were rather vague—close to Princess Street, behind the Parsi Temple—but I felt confident I would be able to find them.

I was hot and sticky as I waited at the bus stop. Nobody seemed to care when, or even if, the bus would come. Heat was only half the problem; poor health was the other. Our Peace Corps group had the dubious distinction of having the worst health record since the agency's inception three years before, and although I had been doing my share in establishing this record, I'd been enjoying a spell of wellness during the previous few weeks. It was hard for me to guess how those around me were feeling; they were quietly patient, conserving energy.

I stood in the bus queue, envying the cow occupying most of the shade offered by the bus stand. The cow was weak, dehydrated, and very bony. Those in line with me were weak, dehydrated, and very bony. As I waited, I wondered whether I was the only one who thought the cow should move or at least share a bit of the shade.

When the bus finally arrived, it was a "standee" bus, and because there were no seats, most of us were able to squash on. With only intimate space available, I was thankful that perspiration was not glue. Unable to move, I thought of myself as an ingredient in a thick stew with lots of garlic, onion, and pungent spices.

The bus chugged along, weaving its way through the dense collection of people, rickshaws, taxis, and other obstacles that cluttered the road. It swerved to avoid hitting a matchstick woman draped in a dusty green sari who was leading a cow. Although Hindus do not eat beef, the cow provides nourishment from milk and fuel from dung. Its sacred status has existed over the centuries. I watched as the woman took a coin from a young man in exchange for a handful of grass plucked from the stack balanced on her head. This was how she made her living. Although the man paid for the privilege of feeding the revered cow, some just touch it and then their heart, head, or both and moved on.

Extracting myself from the bus near Princess Street, I looked for a space where I could get my bearings. Because I wasn't sure where I was going, I didn't consider myself lost. I asked directions from those in the slow-moving stream of humanity. I was fairly proficient in Indian English, but my Hindi was fragile, and my Marathi nonexistent. In any case, there seemed to be no translation for "welfare center." The more queries I made, the more options I had. People responded as if they understood what I was asking. I thanked them as if I understood what they were telling me. Using the law of averages, I went in the direction most frequently suggested.

The earth's halitosis produced by mounds of marinated garbage assaulted me. I became aware of how dehydrated I'd become and was beginning to feel faint. As I wandered around, the old adage often quoted during the British era kept playing over and over in my head: "Only mad dogs and Englishmen go out in the noonday sun."

As I came around the corner, my dazed state was interrupted by the sight of a freshly painted building. It was uncluttered by human existence and protected by an iron gate. Behind the gate, cleanly swept steps led up to a lone watchman standing guard. I climbed the steps and asked to see the Johnsons.

The watchman hesitated for a moment before patting the air with his hand, indicating that I should wait. He then turned and vanished into the building's dark interior. I found the setting oddly still and wondered whether they sent people away during part of the day. It certainly was a strange welfare center. Suddenly two men appeared, evaluated me with suspicious looks, and then they too disappeared into the darkness.

My nature favors impatience, but in India waiting had become a predictable activity. I practiced being rather than doing until the watchman returned and motioned for me to follow him. It was so dark I could barely see and almost bumped into my escort when he stopped abruptly. He stepped aside and waved a hand of introduction to a line of peering eyes placed in the silhouettes of half a dozen men.

My entrance into the room initiated garbled chatter— not Hindi, not Marathi. It took me a few seconds to realize the sounds were various pronunciations of Johnson. A rhythm developed, and soon I was listening to a cacophony of "Johnson, Johnson." As my eyes adjusted, features flowed into the faces of the silhouettes. I sensed from their expressions that they were clearly befuddled.

They pointed to the wall behind me, prompting me to turn around. In the center of the cement wall, I saw something that looked a little like a thermostat. I presumed it was an intercom and shook my head in disbelief. With all of India's needs, why did they spend money on an intercom, which at best probably only worked about twenty percent of the time. Why couldn't one of the men staring at me just go to tell the Johnsons that someone was here to see them? I no longer asked obvious questions, as they seldom rendered meaningful answers.

Aware of my serious audience, I walked to the intercom, prepared to give a good performance. Confidently, I pulled the lever attached to the small metal box. I assumed I was going to have to shout through the three-inch opening. I stepped closer to speak, or shout as the case may be, but what filled my eyes took away all words.

Looking through the opening, I found myself staring down at the remains of a body being eaten by flames. Fragments of bones were still recognizable. I wondered about the person whose final chapter I was witnessing. Was it a life that was being grieved by family and friends, or was it one of an unknown beggar who became lost in the edges of society, died alone, and was collected off the street? There were no clues. In either case, the death would be understood as part of an ongoing cycle, with the unseen soul now free to reincarnate.

My thoughts gave way to the now-sporadic "Johnsons, Johnsons" that continued behind me. I tried to compose myself, afraid that inappropriate laughter might erupt from me at any moment. How could I have made such a mistake! I instantly realized why there were no people around, why it was so quiet, and why the men were so confused. Women were not allowed in crematoriums, unless they were dead. While the untouchables, responsible for handling the dead, puzzled over my presence, I pondered the irony that "untouchables" were the last to touch bodies.

I turned and addressed my perplexed audience. I shook my head back and forth, forgetting that this meant "yes" to most Indians. Aided by hand gestures, I announced, "There's been a mistake. This cremation is not the Johnsons." My conclusion, understood or not, did nothing to sway my audience. Knowing there was no way I could convince them otherwise, or that it really made any difference, I respectfully backed my way through the doorway. With my eyes now adjusted, I was able to see the flatbeds on rollers, which were used to take bodies on their last journey.

My entourage accompanied me to the top of the steps. I nodded my head over prayerful hands and thanked them for allowing me to enter. I felt their eyes follow me as I descended the steps. My own eyes focused on the crowds of people now distilled into individuals, each making his or her own way toward death.

At the bus stop, tattered children with old faces and outstretched hands surrounded me. Their haunting looks told me they knew more about death than I did. I made faces to change theirs, to make them laugh, and they did. They skipped and danced around me and for a few moments forgot their occupation of begging. I boarded the bus and through the window watched them as they went back to work. When they were out of sight, my thoughts returned to the day's experience; it was not what I'd expected, but then in India, nothing ever is.

TICKET PLEASE

*Bombay Train Station: traveling by train
was always an adventure in India*

I wanted to visit the ancient caves of Ajanta and Ellora located near Aurangabad, 200 miles north of Bombay. With that destination in mind, my agenda for the day was to buy a third-class train ticket. The task seemed simple enough, but in the mid-1960s nothing in India was ever simple. Space on all public transport was limited, and often it was easier to walk than to deal with the challenge of trying to get on a bus. Local trains, also stuffed with people, were decorated with men dangling on the sides and gripping the bars on the windows. This was done both for sport and out of necessity. In either case the outcome was sometimes fatal.

Because my planned excursion would fall on one of the twenty-two national holidays celebrated in India, I needed to purchase my ticket far in advance. "Third-class" and "seat" don't belong in the same sentence. Even so, there was a rumor circulating in my Peace Corps group that a daily air-conditioned third-class train from Bombay to Aurangabad not only existed but had assigned seats!

By this time I was living on Girgaum Road, closer to the center of Bombay than Worli. My ration of water still came at 5:30 a.m., and on my ticket-purchasing day, the alarm of water sputtering from the spigot woke me. After filling two buckets, I peered out the window and observed the families living below. Looking down at them, I was reminded of the only instruction my landlord had given me when I moved in a few months before: "Don't throw garbage this window or you hit people, throw this window," he'd said, as he pointed a bony finger to the window on the other side of the room.

Ever prompt, at 5:30 my nine-year-old sweeper, Dusbi, arrived and handed me my daily cup of hot milk tea and an egg, which I had negotiated as part of my lease. He looked so sleepy. I thought about feeling guilty, but didn't. I knew he was happy to trade sleep for the status he gained in his community by working for me.

As a sweeper, he had no ladder of success to climb in this life. Cows were treated with more respect than those of his caste. I sat and drank my tea as I watched him perform his chore. Periodically he would flash me a shy smile, indicating that he appreciated being seen and not being seen through. He always conducted himself professionally and took pride in his work. And almost always, when he left, I gave him my egg and was rewarded with another sleepy smile.

After Dusbi left, I dressed quickly, as I wanted to get an early start to beat the heat. This was only an expression: the heat always won. I cautiously made my way down the permanently dark stairwell so I wouldn't trip over anyone sleeping on the landings. The ground floor was already alive with activity. I could make out the shadows of the boys from the Bombay Dyeing Co. folding and stacking cloth that would be delivered later in the day to shops throughout the city. As I walked though the communal space, the workers acted as though I was invisible, although I knew, and they knew I knew, that all eyes were watching my every step. In such settings, it was as close as I ever got to privacy.

Exiting the building, I joined the already bustling throng of people on Girgaum Road. It took talent to walk the streets of Bombay. I walked quickly and skillfully, navigating my way around people, cows, and bullock carts. I dodged bicycles and rickshaws and looked the other way when I saw the neighborhood's legless leper gaining momentum as he came toward me on his plywood scooter.

The clattering noises of life in progress were accompanied by smells ranging from the delicious aromas of pungent curries to rotting garbage. All were packaged in steamy heat and decorated with colorful saris swishing through the crowds.

By the time I reached Princess Street, pedestrian traffic was moving predominantly in one direction. I joined the stream of humanity and let the current carry me down to Church Gate Station. The ticket office was across the street from the station, and I was pleased to find a relatively short queue for tickets. When my turn came, the ticket attendant, who appeared to be informed, told me in a singsong fashion, "You must be going to VT (Victoria Terminus) for ticket."

I felt the weight of humid heat as I trudged over to VT, where I hoped there would be a "Ladies Line," which would help in expediting my purchase. No such luck. Instead I joined one of the long queues of patient servants content to spend hours in line to buy tickets for others.

There was so much to see and observe—a graduate course in witnessing life in progress. I was amusing myself by counting the number of men who had coins stuck in their ears when a loud crash suddenly interrupted my survey. I turned to see large chunks of the ceiling clattering to the floor. Two men, not twenty feet from me, were clobbered by the ceiling. One appeared relatively unharmed and moved his sleeping mat to another section of the station. The other, bleeding and wailing, was led away by an attendant. In the States one would probably sue. In India someone attacked by a ceiling was more likely to ponder why it was he who had been hit rather than someone else.

When I finally arrived at the front of the queue, I was directed to another queue, and then another. Eventually, I found myself back at the same ticket office near Church Gate where I'd started in the morning. Upon arriving, I spied the man I held responsible for sabotaging my day. I was hot, tired, and very frustrated. Afraid I might lose sight of him, I shouted as I crossed the room, "Why did you send me to VT this morning? I have been there for hours. All I want is a ticket to Aurangabad! How can that be so difficult?"

It bothered me enormously that he was so unmoved. Standing there in his dusty khaki uniform, he appeared to have no remorse whatsoever for squandering my day. He waited patiently until I finished and then, in his sing-song voice, gave me a philosophical response, "Maybe it's not meant for you to go to Aurangabad. You people in the West rush around as if you have only one lifetime. We have all of eternity. Maybe it's not meant for you to go to Aurangabad."

The men in the ticket line watched to see how I would react. I had become their entertainment. I went from being filled with words to having none. My frustration ebbed a little and was replaced with quiet resignation, along with the realization that I wouldn't be getting a ticket that day. I was spent and the day was spent.

On the walk back home, both the day and I became a little cooler. I almost smiled thinking of the most recent lesson India had taught me: some things are not meant to be.

EVALUATING SUCCESS AS A PEACE CORPS VOLUNTEER

Our pilot UCD group breaks up with laughter when the cow decides to relieve itself. (Left to right: Ann Friesen, Swamy, Gerry McColloch, David Langdon, Keekee Minor, Bob Ungerleider)

India XXIII was the first, and last, Peace Corps group to undertake an Urban Community Development (UCD) program in India. Melody and I had been living in the Worli chawls for six months, and although embedded in the community, I can truthfully say that we were total failures at implementing any programs that would help improve the lives of those in our community.

It was 1966, less than twenty years since the British left India. Many Indians equated the English-speaking Peace Corps volunteers with their former British rulers. When they saw us cleaning and scrubbing our floors, they looked on in amused astonishment. This chore was done by sweepers, who ranked only slightly above untouchables responsible for cremating bodies.

Indian social workers, and others in positions somewhat related to ours, generally did not live in the communities where they worked. They felt it diminished their status and made them less effective. I daresay that in my case, it wouldn't have made any difference where I lived.

I had anticipated barriers to implementing a UCD program in India. First of all, we volunteers came from outside the culture; secondly, we were in all in our twenties, giving us little standing in a culture that valued and took guidance from elders. I also had not considered the rationale of karma. A man in a lower caste told me he did not want to become involved with making any changes, as he was afraid it might interfere with future incarnations. He believed the circumstances in his present life were in payment for deeds committed in previous lives. By accepting his currently prescribed life, he would have a better chance of obtaining a higher status when he reincarnated the next time.

These drawbacks were compounded by my inability to speak the language. During our training, at the request of the Indian government, we were taught Hindi, which had recently been declared the national language. But Marathi was the primary language spoken in Bombay, and so by default, charades became my language of choice. In addition to these challenges, changes in India occurred very slowly, and generally little happened unless bribes were paid. It was part of the culture.

By the end of six months, most volunteers were in structured jobs such as teaching, but six of us decided to give UCD another chance. We found a potential site—a municipal housing project in Malad. The site, located in the suburbs of Bombay, had been designated as part of Bombay's slum-clearance program. When we met with community members, they raised an issue they thought we could help with. The problem was with their housing. Their roofs and doors, constructed from pressboard, were disintegrating in the monsoon rains.

Many residents were teachers who spoke English, which was a real plus because the success of any UCD program relies heavily on clear communication. The residents, along with local officials, enthusiastically endorsed our willingness to assist them. All parties concerned agreed that Malad was a good choice for the UCD program's second chance.

Peace Corps staff gave the six of us permission to move into the Peace Corps hostel on Pedder Road while we waited for final approval from the municipal commissioner. We were optimistic that approval would be forthcoming but decided it would be prudent to use our waiting time to locate a back-up site, just in case. Quickly is not an adverb I would ever use to describe how things got done in India, and by the time we finally met with the municipal commissioner six weeks later, our optimism had drained away. We were disappointed, but not surprised, to learn that the project had not been approved.

The commissioner started by saying that he was familiar with the Malad community. Its members were very political and were pushing hard to get the government to fix their housing. He went on to tell us that Indira Gandhi, who was the prime minister of India from 1966–77, had become involved, and there was a fast until death underway in the community until the situation could be resolved. He said we could pick any other site in or around Bombay except that one. (Clearly, the teachers were doing just fine without our help!)

Fortunately, by then we had a Plan B. We had visited a number of areas and agreed on Parsi Wadi, a hutment community on the outskirts of Ghatkopar. The shantytown of five to ten thousand, depending on where you marked the boundary, was located on the Bombay-Agra Road. The population included Hindus from Maharashtra and various northern states, a number of Muslims, and a few Christians. Lots of languages, but not much English.

The director of the Children's Aid Society invited us to work in conjunction with his program in that area, and the chairman of Parsi Wadi's Youth Association also gave his full support. There was another important reason for choosing the site: A man in the community generously offered us a piece of land on which we could build a model hutment for our small Peace Corps group.

During the hiatus between the Malad and Parsi Wadi sites, I'd met an Indian architect, Mohanty, who was interested in designing a prototype hutment. It would use more durable materials and cost less than those commonly constructed from pieces of recycled wood, corrugated metal, and plastic sheets. Residents in the area claimed that the average cost to build a hutment was fifteen rupees (two dollars) a square foot. Mohanty estimated that his design could be built for ten rupees a square foot, two-thirds the cost. When he visited Parsi Wadi, he thought it was a perfect location to build his model and viewed the undertaking as a good way to advertise. He was so excited about the project that he agreed that his firm, Mohanty and Ezra, would provide its services pro bono.

The hutment designed was 484 square feet and included a bathroom. Peace Corps Bombay, Delhi, and Washington all approved the project and agreed to underwrite the cost of construction with three job performance grants of two thousand rupees each. The builder was also on board and signed a statement promising to underwrite any costs exceeding six thousand rupees.

Although the construction of our new home was expected to take three to four weeks, we thought it worth the wait. Not only would we be part of a project illustrating how to build a better hutment, but we would also be able to live in the community.

While we waited for the details to be worked out, we moved into Wadia Estates, built originally to house Sindhi refugees from Pakistan. It was in Kurla, near the airport and about a mile walking distance from Parsi Wadi. Our two rooms were similar to the one Melody and I had shared in Worli. Melody, Ann, and I initially shared one room. In the room the three fellows shared, there was a fourth occupant, Swamy, our cook.

Living in these chawls was different from those in Worli. There we had had some semblance of privacy; in Kurla we had none. Unless it was night, or an extremely intense monsoon rain, we left our doors open. Neighbors would wander in from the floor's connecting balcony. They were not shy about picking up and inspecting various items. Clearly it was an open-door policy.

One day in conversation with a woman in the adjacent room, I asked what her husband did. She said, "Robber." Apparently, he and others would go down to the docks to steal items that were being imported. If they saw someone looking at them suspiciously and were afraid they might be caught, they just dumped the evidence into the Arabian Sea. I'm not sure what other kinds of shady dealings were going on in the area, but given the clientele, I am pretty sure there were no white-collar crimes being committed. People did what they did in order to survive.

The weeks of waiting for approval to build turned into months. By then I had learned that everything in India took an enormous amount of time. It would take forty minutes to cash a check, as the manager would want me to join him for tea. It would take two and a half hours to send a package. First, I would wait in line to have a package weighed. Then I would wait in another queue to buy stamps. The wait in the third and final line was to watch the stamps actually franked. It was known that unfranked stamps were often removed and resold.

This time around we decided to use our waiting time to improve our language skills. We hired a teacher but discontinued classes when he became ill with hepatitis. Some days we spent in futile attempts to make our way through the government's bureaucracy. As time passed, our optimism again faded.

Harsh monsoon rains replaced sunny days, adding another challenge to our daily existence. Trekking over to Parsi Wadi in the pouring rain no longer seemed meaningful, and our visits became less frequent. We rationalized that it would be better to wait until we moved into the community to assess existing problems. On some days I never even left Kurla. To be fair, when weather was severe, Indians did not go to work either. Postal workers went on strike during the monsoon, demanding that they be issued umbrellas. Just existing seemed to be work enough.

We had been on hold for almost four months when we learned that the plot of land promised to us had been in dispute for twelve years! The owner's generous offer had been motivated by his interest in getting us involved so we could help him obtain approval for a dubious development scheme. We acknowledged defeat and accepted the fact that we had failed yet again to implement a UCD program. Nine months, the length of a pregnancy, had passed since our arrival in India, and we were left with a stillbirth. Peace Corps staff sympathized with our predicament and told us to go find jobs and lodging and keep them informed as to what we were up to. Rather than being upset by the outcome, I was ready for a new adventure. By then I had learned to view the challenges and dead ends as inherent Indian realities.

Although I knew I would miss our small group, we all felt it was time to move on. Melody decided to return to the States. David left Bombay for Aurangabad, a more rural area, where he thought community development might have a better chance of succeeding. Gerry stayed in the area and moved in with a family near Parsi Wadi. Bob arranged to work with Tata Industries, and Ann and I ended up working under the auspices of the Nirmala Niketan College of Social Work. Our assigned area was the Goan community of Dhobitalao, located in downtown Bombay.

We found lodging with a family a block away, opposite the Parsi Temple on Girgaum Road. Our arrangement included a sweeper, a daily egg, and bed-tea in the morning. The family had the whole third floor; they moved into one room so Ann and I could each have our own room. I loved having more living space, a luxury some could not relate to.

On one occasion I invited a family from the neighborhood to visit. When they discovered I had a room all to myself, they offered to have some family members come stay with me so I wouldn't be lonely. I explained that in the United States, many people had their own rooms. It was as hard for me to comprehend that they would want to live in a room cluttered with people as it was for them to understand that I liked having a room all to myself.

The challenges of arranging for a new working situation and housing had been solved, but language remained a problem. In Worli, the primary language was Marathi; in Kurla, Farsi; in Parsi Wadi, Urdu and Marathi; and in Dhobitalao, Konkani. The family I rented from spoke Gujarati and a little English. With my minimal linguistic abilities, I attempted to communicate with my landlord and his wife. We had a good laugh when they complimented me on how well I spoke Gujarati, and I confessed, "I'm not speaking Gujarati; I'm speaking Hindi."

Fortunately for me, because I had all but given up on trying to learn any language, many residents in Dhobitalao spoke English. Most in the community were originally from Goa, which had remained a Portuguese territory for centuries until it was annexed by India in 1961. But even with this language advantage, my lack of success in implementing UCD continued.

A final attempt at getting local residents involved with solving a problem occurred when I visited with a family on the top floor of one of the buildings. A couple of umbrellas hung upside down from their ceiling. I thought of them as black chandeliers, but their function was to catch water dripping through the roof. I asked them why they hadn't demanded to get the roof fixed, withhold their rent...something! They laughed and assured me it would do no good but agreed to file a complaint. Quite honestly, their willingness to do so was to please me. I'm sure they thought me naive, and on some level, by then even I knew it would be a useless effort. A month later, they proudly told me they had filed a complaint and the hearing was scheduled to come up in nine years, which translated into never. I was much more discouraged than they were.

Although I'd had a string of failures over the year and a half I had been in Bombay, the activity of just living took a lot of time and energy. Because Ann and I had no cook and no refrigeration, on most mornings I went to Crawford Market a few blocks away to buy food. There I would find coolies sitting in their baskets. The baskets were the tools of their trade, used to collect produce for customers shopping in the market. Initially, the coolies jumped up and ran after me, but when they figured out that I carried my own purchases, they just waved and smiled as I passed. There was a fine line between being seen as entertainment and showing another way of life by example.

Just taking care of everyday needs filled my days. I visited with those in the community but no longer had any illusions that I was a change agent. Making meaningful changes in urban India was an assignment that was way beyond my capabilities. Mahatma Gandhi succeeded, but I was no Gandhi.

One day, as I was talking with a resident in Dhobitalao, I realized that he should be at work. When I asked him why he wasn't, he casually responded, "Why would I go to work if you're here to talk to?" My initial instinct was to disagree, but then I decided he was right—there would always be time for work. I quickly gave up feeling guilty about detaining him, and we continued to talk and exchange ideas and information. After all, learning about each other's culture was one of the Peace Corps' three goals.

Another goal was to provide technical skills and, hopefully, leave behind an infrastructure so that projects started in partnership with local residents could continue. Urban Community Development came under this goal.

The third goal of the Peace Corps was to be realized when volunteers returned home. They were to share their experiences with others and incorporate the lessons they learned into their own future endeavors.

Today, as I reflect on my experiences as a volunteer, I know I was not successful in carrying out the goal of imparting technical skills. And I am unable to evaluate the level of impact I may have had on others after returning home. As for the goal of shrinking the world by interacting with and appreciating other cultures, if I changed the acronym UCD from Urban Community Development to Understanding Cultural Differences, I think I, and those in my group, could claim success.

SIKKIM: A HIMALAYAN KINGDOM

*After I crossed the washed-out
road on returning from Sikkim
to India, others followed*

After serving two years as a Peace Corps Volunteer in
Bombay, I was content to have my itinerary evolve as I
meandered east toward the little-known country of Sikkim,
a tiny Himalayan kingdom squeezed in between India and
China. My knowledge of the country was limited. I knew

the queen was American and that getting a permit to enter the country was next to impossible, but I like a challenge. As part of a 1950 treaty, the Indian government, a bureaucracy synonymous with sticky red tape, was responsible for issuing permits, in lieu of visas, for Sikkim.

The monsoon rains and I left Bombay and made our way northeast across the country toward Darjeeling. Through the windows of trains and buses, I marveled at how the rains repainted the landscape. For nine months each year the sun beats down, cracking the earth's surface and turning it to dust. Unrelenting rays burn color from the countryside until it looks like an overexposed photo. Then, when heavy gray clouds displace the sun and torrential rains flood the fields, the landscape becomes freshly painted with bright-green vegetation. Men, women, and children become giddy with delight when the monsoon presents herself, a celebrity making a grand entrance. But all too soon she wears out her welcome with mud, mold, and mildew.

It took about a week to get to Darjeeling. Upon my arrival I rummaged through my rucksack and located the letter of introduction a Peace Corps friend had given me before I left Bombay. The address was for the Bethany School, an orphanage for young girls. I presented the letter and myself to the nun who opened the door. She seemed both surprised and composed. "Wait here," she said before bustling away with my letter. While waiting I divided my attention between smelling the strong aroma of curry cooking—I was hungry—and watching a child of ten or so peer around a side door. She giggled, disappeared, and then returned with other giggling children.

A few minutes later, Mrs. Bagalos, a matronly woman wearing both a smile and a worried look, arrived. Although not dressed in the traditional black-and-white habit, she was clearly the one in charge. After some discussion with her staff, Mrs. Bagalos said I could stay in the common room. Five rupees (less than fifty cents) a day covered the cost of my room, three meals, and two teas.

I quickly folded into the routine of the school, meaning I showed up for most meals and teas. In the mornings I would go to the deputy commissioner's office to see whether my permit for Sikkim had arrived. The Indian authorities informed me it would take a very long time for me to get a permit, and it was quite possible I would never get one. Never is a long time, even in India. I felt sure this delay tactic was their way of asking for *baksheesh* (a bribe), but I feigned ignorance and assured them I was prepared to wait indefinitely.

After that daily chore, I'd generally wander around in the rain observing life. Sometimes I'd stop for tea at the Windermere, an old English hotel aging with grace, where the American debutante Hope Cooke was said to have been staying when she met her future husband, the *Chogyal* (king) of Sikkim. It seemed an appropriate setting for the beginning of a fairy tale.

In addition to my walkabouts, I accompanied a Canadian nurse to a nearby temple, where she provided medical care to Tibetan refugees. They had wrinkled, weather-beaten faces, and as I observed them patiently waiting in line, I thought about the struggles they must have gone through in escaping the Chinese takeover of Tibet.

One day, I cut the hair of some children from a nearby orphanage. It was a rather festive occasion, held outside on one of the few days it didn't rain. The children would take turns occupying the various chairs scattered about the yard. Although I didn't think I'd done any worse than the other surrogate barbers, I must admit many of the children looked better before their hair was shorn.

My permit arrived on September 16, about two weeks after my arrival. It was also the day that I first heard rumors about fighting taking place on the border between Sikkim and the Tibetan region of China. The news prompted me to make arrangements for an immediate departure, as I knew it was only a matter of time before the border between India and Sikkim would be closed.

When I informed Mrs. Bagalso that I would be leaving the following day, she insisted on lending me an umbrella and sweater. I left behind most of my belongings packed neatly in my rucksack and promised the cloistered staff that I would share my adventures with them when I returned. The next morning, the nuns huddled together in the frame of the front door to wave good-bye. None of them looked as if they wanted to change places with me, but then I wouldn't have wanted to change places with any of them. I was ready, black umbrella in one hand, a drawstring purse the size of a large cantaloupe in the other, and my well-worn bulky sleeping bag tucked under my arm. My flip-flops slapped the wet pavement as I walked toward the taxi stand to catch the next Land Rover headed for Sikkim.

There was no official schedule. Once a Land Rover had a full complement of passengers, it simply left. We stopped at each village along the way to exchange arriving and departing passengers. While we waited for passenger replacements, those continuing on patronized local tea shops. Often a large vat of milk tea would be steaming over an open fire. Shop owners ladled tea into cracked cups and distributed them to those of us who found places to sit at rickety old tables, sheltered by thatched roofs. Many followed the custom of pouring their tea into saucers to cool. Some poured the cooled tea back into their cups, while others slurped it from saucers. The sound of steady pounding rain replaced conversation. I listened to these sounds as I watched water pouring over the edges of the straw roof protecting us.

After our respites, which ranged from five minutes to more than an hour, we piled back into our waiting transport. At each of the three checkpoints, I inquired, "Will you be closing the borders?" The reply was always the same, "Yes, *memsahib*, we will be closing the borders." Each checkpoint had a registration book. I noted in one of them that a German had crossed earlier in the day. The previous entry was August 22, more than three weeks before; five people had registered that day. I knew then that running into a lot of tourists was not going to be a problem.

When we reached Teesta Bridge, on the border between India and Sikkim, our fluid group transferred from a Land Rover to a Jeep. The transition made me smile. Land Rovers served as mementos left by the British Empire, while the Jeep had the fingerprints of one American female, the *Gyalmo* (queen).

After we crossed the bridge, we bumped along on muddy roads that wiggled their way through mountainous hills. Each bend in the road was like turning a page in a book of fairy tales. Fallen clouds shrouded landscapes where monsters could hide. Then, as we rounded curves, the fog would be swept away, leaving behind a panorama of a lush green countryside densely decorated with flowers. I half expected elves to dance across the road. The scenery was a visual mantra, which nurtured my soul.

When the vistas faded into the fog, I turned my attention to my companions, whose eyes periodically gave me a polite peek. Their curious glances ventured out from weathered faces lined with histories I could not read. When I looked in their direction, they invariably looked away. The men were dressed in baggy pants, well-worn shirts, and jackets. The women wore brightly colored Tibetan dresses, full-length garments with both sides folded toward the back and held together with a belt at the waist. Their brightly colored, rough-texture clothing contrasted sharply with their quiet demeanor.

About eighteen miles from Gangtok, the capital of Sikkim, everyone got out except the driver and me. Although I had no idea why it was such a popular stop, I knew that because there were no passengers around, I had a long wait ahead of me. After more than an hour, with no departing passengers presenting themselves, another Jeep arrived. Learning that it too was destined for the capital, I changed transports. There was no discussion, and I was not asked to pay more. I sensed that changing transports was a common practice. My original driver, whom I left sitting on an old wooden bench calmly sipping tea, waved to me as we pulled away.

On this last segment of the trip, I sat next to a Mr. Lama, head of forestry for Sikkim. He gave me his telephone number (51), in case I needed any assistance once we reached Gangtok. His first question to me was, "Are you a reporter?" I assured him I was not, although the activity I'd witnessed throughout the day might have been of interest to reporters. Other than taxis, almost all of the transports were military. His question about my being a reporter stopped me from asking him what the fighting was all about. I did ask him for suggestions on a good place to stay, and he recommended the Denzong Hotel.

I soon found out it was the only hotel, and it was full. Reporters from India, covering the military skirmishes taking place on the border, had taken all five rooms. Bali, the manager of the hotel, assured me that he would find me a place to stay, and he did, at the Soldiers, Sailors, Airmen Receiving Rest House, which was located a short distance from the hotel. Bali was emphatic that no one else would be staying there. I think he thought he was reassuring me. He arranged for a bucket of water to be provided and promised that a watchman would be posted at the building. It sounded too good to be true.

Once my lodging was taken care of, I relaxed and enjoyed the evening in the company of the press corps. The atmosphere was jovial. It was clear that although the reporters were from different agencies, they all knew each other. I was a fresh audience for their well-rehearsed stories. Although many subjects were touched on, the fighting they were sent to cover was never mentioned. At dinner, Mr. Das, the reporter from UPI, casually asked me, "Would you like to meet the king? I can arrange it." Of course I said yes, thinking that my magical day was ending perfectly.

But the day hadn't quite ended. Blackout restrictions were in effect, and total blackness greeted me as I left the hotel. I returned and got a flashlight from Bali. The darkness swallowed everything, leaving only an eerie silence, interrupted once by a Jeep passing by. I presumed it was returning from the front, which I'd been told at dinner was only thirteen miles away "as the crow flies." I crept along as though I might fall off the edge of the earth.

When I finally arrived at my lodging, a bucket of water stood patiently next to the door. It was no surprise that the promised watchman was not there. The door was ajar and squeaked loudly as I gently pushed it open. It was downright spooky. I shuffled around until I found the stairs and climbed them, hesitating after each whiny step. Reaching the top, I turned on the flashlight for a few seconds to get a peek at the room to the right. In a flash I saw a bed, a chair, a table, and a glass that could serve as a toilet if I needed it during the night. Perfect.

I unrolled my sleeping bag and bunched up the clothes that were wrapped inside to make a nice pillow. A few items, such as my toothbrush, clattered to the floor, but because I did not hear rats scurrying about, I assumed that my belongings would be safe until morning.

I snuggled down into my sleeping bag and listened to the sporadic sound of artillery in the distance; then all went quiet, very quiet. My thoughts seemed loud in the silence. Would I really get to meet the king? What would I wear!? As I had only one dress, the question had only one answer. The dress was a green-and-gold-marbled nylon shift I had bought in Venice during my hitchhiking days. The well-traveled garment doubled as a nightgown and rolled up into nothing. I would wear it, my flip-flops, and the borrowed sweater. Not a Cinderella look, but then a frilly ballroom dress would have been equally inappropriate.

When I arrived at the hotel for breakfast the next morning, Bali told me that the reporters had already gone and had left me one of the two Jeeps allocated for their use. With the Jeep came a driver and a guide. I did not have a Cinderella persona, but I had a coach, driver, and footman.

I didn't have an answer when Bali asked me where I would like to go but thought a little preparation was in order in case the royal visit materialized. After some discussion he proposed I go to the office of Mr. Rai, head of publicity for Sikkim. My coach arrived after breakfast, and my assigned guide directed the driver to Mr. Rai's office.

Scanning some brochures, I learned that Sikkim was about the size of Delaware, with a population of 170,000. The annual per capita income was nine hundred rupees. There were sixty-seven monasteries; the state religion was Mahayana Buddhism. The spice cardamom was a major export. Included in the four thousand varieties of flowering plants and shrubs were five hundred species of orchids indigenous to Sikkim.

Mr. Rai and his staff of one acknowledged that the queen was influential in certain areas. She had contributed substantially to strengthening the school system and had taken a great deal of interest in cottage-industry crafts. He praised her efforts in these areas, but he was clearly less enthusiastic and more guarded in his remarks relating to her influence in governmental affairs. As if he were reassuring himself, he put it in perspective: "The king has been married before, and the heir to the throne will not be from this current marriage."

After my briefing, I asked to visit the girls' school, a rather unimaginable option, given that I've always tried to keep my distance from schools. But it was an interest of the queen's and therefore a prudent choice. Upon my arrival I learned that one of the teachers was sick. I felt a sense of power and pleasure when I dispatched the driver to take her home. When he returned, we went off to the boys' school. Captain Naryan, whom I had met the night before at the hotel, showed me around. Because books and other props for learning were imported from the United States for both schools, I wondered about the relevance of some of the materials.

My last stop of the morning was the cottage-industry craft shop. I bought two batiks, one green Tibetan dress, a belt, and four bamboo bangles with dragons painted on them. My contribution to the local economy was $14.80.

I returned to the Denzong Hotel too late for lunch but in time to join the reporters for tea. Mr. Das told me he had made arrangements for me to meet the king and queen at six that evening. While we were having tea, the secretary of the board overseeing the rest house where I was staying joined us. He told me the rest house was primarily for visiting dignitaries. I was unable to ascertain from his remark whether he thought I was a dignitary or an exception. When he found out I was meeting the king and queen, he suggested I present them with a *khata*, a scarf. It was an old Tibetan custom.

He explained, "Present to the Chogyal first. He will give it back. Then give it to the Gyalmo. She will return it for you to keep. The quality of the material is not important, but tradition is." Illustrating with a napkin, he showed me how to fold the scarf so it would unfurl easily.

That afternoon I went to the shopping area, where a string of stalls lived under makeshift canopies. People would bow to me as they passed. Although it made me feel a little funny, I accepted it as a proxy gesture usually reserved for the king and queen. I nodded back as if to release them from their duty. I enjoyed bargaining with the shopkeepers and bought boots for the next leg of my trip, trekking in Nepal. Having already spent a lot of money at the craft shop in the morning, I purchased cheesecloth for the evening's Tibetan greeting ritual.

At the appointed hour, my driver for the day picked me up and took me to the palace, a big white house with a red roof. Prayer flags lined the front yard and flapped in the rain. Because the driver dropped me at the side of the building, I entered through the kitchen. Maybe that was fitting. I looked a little forlorn in my dated dress with a few holes, which I didn't think showed too much because of the pattern. On the other hand, my rubber flip-flops had no place to hide. And the sweater hardly cloaked the sins of the outfit, as I had discovered a scorched area on the back when I put it on.

When I entered the large living room, the king and queen, in traditional Tibetan dress, stood ready to receive me at the other end. Through the window that framed them, prayer flags waved in the background for attention.

A few people sat in front of the window. Realizing all eyes were on me, I assumed it was the appropriate moment to get the scarf out. My umbrella promptly fell over when I leaned it against one of the royal tables. Because my purse opened with drawstrings, I put it on the floor in order to dig out the scarf more easily. I was painfully conscious of how polite and patient my royal hosts were. I located and pulled the scarf free, but it did not unfurl as had been demonstrated by my instructor. Rather, it wadded up into a cheesecloth ball. If I had been watching all this, I probably would have laughed, but no one did, and I performed in embarrassing silence.

I regretted not spending a little more to get a proper scarf. After untangling the cloth, I presented what looked like a rag to the king, who reminded me of the seasoned Tibetan monk I had met in Darjeeling. He handed the tattered material back and said, "Hi." That was a shock! I expected him to say "Namaste," or even "Hello," but "Hi!"

I then presented the cheesecloth to the queen, who seemed to be about my age—mid-twenties. She returned it and in a tiny soft voice invited me to sit down. I proceeded to sit down on a telephone that was hidden under a pillow but pretended not to notice.

The king sat next to me; to his left was Steve Lal, a very handsome young man whose father had been the *Diwan* (prime minister) of Sikkim. To his left was Alice, a friend of the queen's from New York. Seated to my right was a general and his wife, and to their right, the queen. After introductions, we all selected glasses from a tray before giving drink orders. When I ordered a gin and tonic, the king said, "Then you're taking the wrong glass." I began to wonder how many more faux pas I would commit throughout the evening.

In spite of my shaky beginning, I was made to feel welcome. The initial stream of questions revolved around how I'd been able to get a permit and how long it had taken. Actually, they were amazed I'd been able to get a permit at all. They were interested in having people visit Sikkim and quizzed me about whether people were interested in doing so. The queen was particularly perturbed when I mentioned that the Peace Corps discouraged volunteers from visiting because of the country's proximity to the Chinese border. They all agreed that India intentionally delayed issuing permits under the pretense that they were protecting the country, when in reality they were controlling it.

We switched from that reality to what I considered a real fantasy, even for a king. He wanted an international airport built! Even if India permitted it, I doubted there was any place level enough in the entire country to accommodate a landing strip. The king became very excited during this discussion. He stuttered and then couldn't speak at all. He squinted his eyes closed, held his breath, as I held mine, and we all waited until he was able to speak again.

We moved on to other subjects. Steve asked me, "So what are you going to do with the boots you bought in the bazaar today?" Surprised, I responded, "How did you know I bought boots?" Laughter: "Didn't you notice the crowd following you? Everybody knows everything you're doing." For some it seemed, I was more of a happening than the war.

The king, keeping abreast of what was happening in the world, asked me, "Are you a hippie?" I responded, "I don't think so." I'd been away from the States for so long I wasn't sure what he was talking about.

We chatted about the war in such vague terms that my ignorance remained unthreatened. More concrete and understandable were comments relating to how difficult it was to put on a Tibetan dress without assistance and how Sikkim inspired one to write poetry. The king, admiring the dragon bangles I'd bought in the market, announced that he thought he'd get some. "Sorry, you're too late," I said. "I bought the last four." His reply: "That's OK, I'll have them make more. After all, I'm the King." I knew then I was inside a fairy tale!

We compared prices between what I paid at the craft shop with what I might have paid in India. Based on this information, the king suggested to the queen that prices should be raised. I wondered how relevant the discussion was because they had virtually no tourists. Then again, because I was in a make-believe story, why shouldn't they pretend too?

At one point, when I took it upon myself to offer additional ice for the glasses, the king said, "I never refuse a beautiful woman." All conversation stopped. Knowing how I looked, I assumed he was tipsy. Fortunately a diversion arrived in the form of a young prince, who came zipping into the room on his bike. He then attempted, unsuccessfully, to stand on his head. I remembered Mr. Das telling me the previous evening that he'd been with the King shortly before the birth of this son and had asked him if he was excited about the upcoming event. He quoted the King's response: "No, it's her first, but not mine."

Three men arrived and prostrated themselves before the King, who dismissed them with a wave of the hand. I decided the men's arrival was my cue to leave. My offer to drop the general and his wife off at their bungalow was graciously accepted.

When I reached the hotel, I joined the members of the press, who were enjoying their own cocktail party. Clearly, drinking was a way of life for them, and although you needed a permit to buy liquor in India, I felt sure they had connections for getting around that legal requirement. In Sikkim there seemed to be no restrictions for alcohol; it was an area of activity the Indians chose not to control.

In the morning bad weather scuttled my plan to go with the reporter from *Life* magazine to a Tibetan monastery. The condition of the roads had deteriorated significantly with the unrelenting rain. The reporter for *Life* said he had decided to leave the country as soon as he could get transport. He was sure it was only a matter of time before the roads would become impassable. I soon learned that all the reporters were making exit plans, and they encouraged me to do the same. Mr. Rai came by to check on me and agreed with the reporters that leaving as quickly as possible was the prudent thing to do. One of the men suggested that my permit should be extended. Others protested, saying that it was "too dangerous" for me to stay on. I didn't think it was "too dangerous," but given everybody's sincere concern for my well-being, I agreed to take the next available vehicle back to India.

Mr. Rai made arrangements for my departure, and I was on my way by 10:30 a.m. As before, the driver stopped to pick up and drop off passengers. Rumor was that there had been a major landslide. In one village a man came up to me and asked, "What are you going to do?" I asked what he meant. He confirmed that the road into India had in fact been washed out. I said I would go have a look and then decide. When I arrived at the scene and looked over the precipice, I realized the whole mountainside had given way. As I stared down at what was now a rushing river, it was hard to determine where the road had been. I spied one of my press friends who was also staring down; he appeared to be pondering his options. He said there was another road connecting Sikkim to India, but he understood it too was washed out.

The man who had approached me earlier in the village came up and asked again, "What are you going to do?" Because his English was perfect, I assumed he had been sent from Gangtok to make sure I was OK. That turned out to be the case. He gave his name, Mr. S. Lama, head of transport for Sikkim. So my fairy tale even had a knight in shining armor, disguised as a middle-aged fatherly type.

When I explained that my permit would expire the following day, he assured me that under the circumstances there would be no problem in extending it. He had been instructed to follow me and take me back to Gangtok, if that was my wish. His Jeep (coach) was at my disposal. I asked how long it would take to rebuild the road. His response: "About ten days." I wondered to myself if that was ten days in Indian time.

Another Jeep arrived from the North, and on the other side, another Land Rover arrived from the South. I felt as if I were on a movie set with no director. Everybody was wandering around, and nobody seemed to know what to do. Finally someone from the other side yelled, "Anyone for Darjeeling?" Having calculated by then that ten days in Indian time might well mean a month, I yelled back, "Yes."

I had made my decision. Mr. Lama arranged for a coolie to go in front of me. Another coolie, carrying my sleeping bag followed behind me. As I slipped down the embankment, outstretched hands kept me from falling. The roaring water compromised communication, so waving hands and pointing fingers replaced inaudible voices. The water wasn't deep, but the mud sucked my feet downward, while the exceedingly strong current tried to sweep me away. Cheers went up on both sides when we made it to the other side.

When I reached the summit and looked back, passengers from both sides were scrambling down the embankments and lining up to take their chances at getting across to the other side. Soon, enough passengers had collected to fill a waiting Land Rover headed for Darjeeling. As we pulled away, I turned to glimpse the last page of my fairy tale. Gazing out the window, I knew in my heart that not only my experience but also the tiny Himalayan kingdom of Sikkim were both destined to survive only in my memories.

*   *   *

Eight years later, in 1975, Sikkim became the twenty-second state of India, and the Himalayan kingdom that had been in existence for over three hundred years came to an end. By definition, fairy tales are supposed to have happy endings. They do, of course, unless reality interferes. Real-world events superseded this Himalayan fairy tale, but because I left in the middle of the story, my memory preserves a happy ending.

Part III

Traveling for Work and Pleasure 1970–90

THE READING OF PALMS AND STARS

My hands painted with henna at pre-wedding party in Bombay in 2004

My first trip back to India after the Peace Corps was in 1971. I spent a week in Bombay before going to Delhi to visit my friend Sarla, whom I had met at a family-planning conference in Chicago. She was working as a liaison between the Indian government and the press, and when I learned that her family's astrologer, Chabbi, was working for the press, I asked whether she could make an appointment for me to have a reading. Although Chabbi's day job was as a reporter, he was better known as an astrologer. He had done readings for Sanjay, Indira Gandhi's oldest son, as well as many other famous people.

Chabbi wasn't in when Sarla and I went to the press office to find him, but by way of endorsement his colleagues related the following story about John Kenneth Galbraith, the esteemed American economist, writer, and lecturer.

When Chabbi was a student at Banaras University in the mid-'50s, he was asked and agreed to take Galbraith for an astrological reading. After the reading, Galbraith returned to the carriage, where Chabbi was waiting for him. Chabbi sensed that Galbraith had been underwhelmed by the experience and asked him to show him his palm. He then proceeded to tell him that he would become internationally well known. Galbraith, not known for his modesty, replied that he was already internationally well known as an academic economist. Chabbi continued, predicting that Galbraith would return to India as the United States' representative. Although Galbraith made no comment about the prediction, he handed Chabbi his business card and said that if he returned to India in such a capacity, Chabbi should present the card to him.

Galbraith became ambassador to India in 1961. When Chabbi met up with him at a press conference, he asked Galbraith whether he remembered him. Not surprisingly, Galbraith did not. That was Chabbi's cue to remove the dog-eared business card from his breast pocket and present it to Galbraith. As memory of their prior meeting returned, Chabbi gave Galbraith another prediction: he would be leaving his current position sooner than planned. Galbraith brushed the prophecy aside as ridiculous. After all he had just arrived in India, and it was expected that he would serve at least through Kennedy's first term. As it turned out, Galbraith left India in July of 1963 after only twenty-seven months as ambassador.

Members of the press recounting the story were discussing whether Chabbi would ask Galbraith, who had recently arrived in India, whether he remembered their second encounter and the prediction of his premature departure.

The following day Sarla tracked down Chabbi and made an appointment for me. During my two years as a Peace Corps volunteer in Bombay, I had not gone to an astrologer, which I consider a cultural oversight. In India it was customary to consult astrologers before making important decisions, such as whether to go into politics, the advisability of making certain investments, whether to change jobs, and comparing charts of those planning to get married to see whether the couple would be a good match. Maybe I didn't go because I was not making any life-altering decisions, or maybe the right opportunity hadn't presented itself.

Although I had not gone to an astrologer, three other Peace Corps volunteers and I had our pasts read by the "shadow man." About four o'clock one afternoon, four of us went to the roof of a building, where the shadow man instructed us where to stand. He then measured the length of our shadows, and based on length alone, he proceeded to tell each of us about our past lives. The experience made an impression, but what he told me must not have, as there are no telling entries in my diary.

I've always had an interest in areas of belief that fall outside the logical realm but generally don't give much credence to advice obtained from such sources. Before leaving on my trip in 1971, I sought out an astrologer in the States to see whether it was a good time to go to India. I was told it was not and was advised not to go. My stay in India happened to coincide with the thirteen-day war between India and Pakistan, resulting in the establishment of Bangladesh. I suppose some would consider that it probably wasn't the best time to go to India, but not me.

Sarla made arrangements for me to meet with Chabbi. At her suggestion I presented him with a few packets of *paan*, which included areca nuts, tobacco, and spices wrapped in betel leaves. Although I thought chewing paan was an unpleasant Indian habit, Chabbi seemed pleased with the offering and placed the paan carefully on the small table next to where he was sitting on the floor in the lotus position.

He came across as a man far more modest than his reputation. After I gave him the date, time, and place of my birth, he asked to look at my palms, which he examined briefly. Taking his time, he adjusted his thick frame, making micro-movements until he settled into a comfortable position. I got the feeling that although outwardly he was adjusting his body, inwardly he was quieting his mind. Once he was comfortable, he ceremoniously reached over, selected one of the packets of paan, placed it on his tongue, and began a slow and rhythmic chewing. Periodically he would wipe away the red betel juice that leaked out of his mouth. Unconsciously, he fiddled with the stained handkerchief in his lap as he looked off into space.

Sarla explained before we arrived that Chabbi would first ask me a couple of questions about my past; the percentage of concurring responses would determine how accurate the reading would be. The questions were specific. His first: "Did you recently receive a pearl ring?" I said, "No." He asked Sarla to repeat the question in case I hadn't understood. I repeated, "No," thinking with amusement that I would certainly know whether I had received a pearl ring. He then asked whether my mother had been ill in January. Again I said, "No." Two nos gave me little hope for the reading. He didn't ask whether I had any particular questions. Instead he rocked back and forth and began speaking, more to the walls and ceiling than to me, seemingly saying whatever came to mind. I would have problems with a tooth, I would be buying a new car, I would be meeting an interesting person connected to the Orient. I listened respectfully but said nothing after denying that I had received a pearl ring.

Chabbi delivered predictions, Sarla translated, and I took notes. I didn't think he had gotten much right: I had excellent teeth, had never bought a new car, and thought meeting someone from the Orient a bit of a stretch. Still, I wasn't disappointed. I felt privileged to have had a reading from the well-known astrologer and appreciated the cultural significance of the experience. What remained perplexing though was the exchange about the pearl ring. It was clear that Chabbi had difficulty in believing I had not received one.

It was while walking through the market a few days later that I inexplicably recalled that in fact I *had* received a pearl ring. The week before I left for India, I had gotten a call from a friend of the family who lived in the Washington, DC, area. She explained that she was calling on behalf of another friend who had known one of my great-uncles decades earlier. He had given her a ring and she, now over 90, felt it should be returned to my mother's family. It arrived through the mail slot of the door with nothing on the envelope but my name. The ring had been an earring, but when its mate was lost, it was made into a ring. In the center of a black onyx, about the size of a penny and trimmed in sculpted gold, was a flower made of five small pearls surrounding a tiny gold center. When Chabbi had said a pearl ring, I had pictured a setting of one or possibly two pearls. But he was correct. One would certainly call it a pearl ring, not a black onyx ring.

Chabbi continued to be right. A week after the reading, while eating an orange, I bit down on a seed and cracked a tooth. This little mishap required a root canal when I returned to the States. As for the Oriental connection, on my return from India I met a man on the plane who traveled exclusively between Japan and the States for business. Over the next few years we would meet either in New York or San Francisco. Furthermore, a month after my return, I was driving back to Washington from Ohio after visiting my parents when my car was rear-ended and jammed into the car in front of me. It was totaled, and yes, I did end up buying a new car. And as for my mother, who was almost never sick, I learned that in fact she had been ill the previous January. Chabbi's accuracy stunned me. The Galbraith story, as well as my own experience, confirmed in my mind that Chabbi's reputation as an astrologer was only a footnote to his ability as a psychic.

As for the ring, it vanished about ten years later. It's as though it came into my life for a purpose, possibly to teach me to have an appreciation for that which defies logic. Once the lesson was learned, there was no longer a need for me to possess the ring. I admit I miss it, and to this day continue to look for it in antique shops. I don't expect to find it, but the looking keeps the memory fresh.

Although I felt my ring experience had come full circle, the validity of stories about Galbraith seemed unconfirmed. So when he came to Chautauqua in the summer of 1986 to give a lecture in the Amphitheater, I accosted him on the brick walk. I'm not sure which one of us was caught more off guard—I, who was somewhat stunned by his towering height, or he, who was being asked to respond to the authenticity of encounters that had taken place over a decade earlier. He was clearly befuddled by my query, but rather than answering, he turned on his heels and strode away in the opposite direction. My own interpretation is that he did recall his encounters with Chabbi but did not want to admit it. He might well have thought that as a serious thinker and renowned academician, acknowledging that he had ever expressed any interest in astrology might undermine his well-established credibility.

Throughout the world, there are those who receive comfort and guidance from the location of planets, lines in the hands, the order of cards, and the position of thrown coins. When it comes to faith and beliefs, each individual must judge and decide for him or herself, how best to view and value those things that exist beyond our five senses.

A Sail through the Bermuda Triangle

*Paul, Keekee, Marv, and Sam, before departing
for Saint Thomas, October 1975*

Four days of good weather. That's what Sam said he wanted before we set sail for Saint Thomas in October, 1975. He had called me in August to see whether I would help him take his boat down to the Caribbean. I'd said yes, remembering that the previous June a psychic in Reno had read my tea leaves and predicted that I would take a trip over water in October. Although at that time I had absolutely no thought of doing so, the memory of that prediction surfaced when Sam called.

The trip felt predestined, and by the time October rolled around I was more than ready. I had just accepted the position as director of field operations for the international division of the Planned Parenthood Federation of America (PPFA). A sailing trip through the Bermuda Triangle seemed like a perfect transition from working for the mainline federal agency, Health, Education, and Welfare (now Health and Human Services) in Washington, to a nonprofit based in New York City.

When I arrived at the dock in Beaufort, North Carolina, Sam had the boat ready. His six weeks of preparation showed. The teak deck of the 42-foot yawl *Fantasy* was polished to a bowling-alley shine. Her freshly painted hull was a soothing sky blue, and new sheets, coiled just so, lay patiently on the deck. Sam had also made a number of meals and put them in the freezer. There was nothing left to do.

The rest of the crew, all from Wisconsin, arrived a few hours later. Marv was an experienced sailor and had sailed with Sam on the Great Lakes. He brought Bobbie, a woman he'd met a couple of weeks before. The other member, Paul, hadn't sailed much. We spent the first evening on deck getting to know each other, and the adage of living in a small world proved true when I discovered I'd taken a computer course from Paul in Chicago in the summer of 1970.

When Sam initially called me about the trip, I'd agreed, providing he didn't drink during the crossing. Because I knew this would be difficult for him, I suggested that Paul and I, the only two who smoked, give up smoking. We saw these commitments as healthy challenges.

The forecast predicted iffy weather, but we couldn't wait and so left the following morning along with a Canadian boat that was moored close by. The sun was shining and the wind was soft. I felt as though we were in a moving postcard. That evening more than two dozen dolphins swam and played around our boat; I wondered if they were entertaining us or if we were entertaining them.

After putting the boat on autopilot, we gathered in the galley for our first meal. During dinner the wind picked up. We turned the engine off and continued under sail. Sam and Paul went to bed fairly early, as it was agreed that Marv would take the first watch. Bobbie disappeared into the fore cabin, and I stayed up on deck with Marv.

Away from the air pollution, I saw the sky as a large black bowl turned upside down and splattered with millions of stars. Looking up, we were able to pick out a number of constellations. Looking down, I watched my hand divide liquid light as it sliced through the phosphorescent water. The setting was magical, but as the night wore on, the passage became rougher. I found being on deck preferable to trying to sleep in the bowels of the boat.

Marv assured me the weather would improve once we got through the Gulf Stream, but by the next afternoon the swells—or "bumps," as we called them—were increasing rather than diminishing in size, and the wind was getting stronger. I'd originally advocated sharing all responsibilities equally, but as my turn to take the helm neared, I realized my skills were grossly inadequate for the task. Marv's comment was that my taking the helm would be equivalent to "learning how to drive in the Indianapolis 500."

For dinner I heated some of the stew Sam had made from scratch and frozen. I burned the pan, so it had a bit of a smoky taste, but nobody complained. We ate in shifts, except for Bobbie, who confined herself to the fore cabin.

The *Fantasy* became a giant roller coaster, climbing up the walls of water and crashing down the other side. To get better control of the boat, the mainsail was reefed down, and the jib was changed frequently. Whoever was at the helm worked hard to keep us from turning broadside. Marv and Sam accurately screamed out the number of minutes before the next squall would hit. We all wore harnesses on deck, religiously clamping ourselves onto the guardrail. We discussed the obvious: that if one of us went overboard, there would be zero chance of that person surviving.

In the cabin I felt as if I were a pinball ricocheting off whatever I slammed into. My bruises were not a pretty sight. The noise was deafening, and because it was almost impossible to hear, we communicated using charades. If it were a movie, there would be a break and a shift to a quieter scene, but there was no relief and no other scene.

Hours turned into days. When the gale force winds finally diminished, we knew we'd seen the worst of it. Marv spotted a Norwegian liner and suggested Sam radio it to check our position. We learned that not only were we way off course, but we had just come through Tropical Storm Hallie.

It was then that Sam acknowledged his navigational skills were somewhat weak. He admitted that when he had practiced plotting courses before leaving Wisconsin, he had ended up in Oklahoma. This news was both funny and unsettling.

I had put myself in charge of watches and for safety reasons stayed up nights with whoever was at the helm. With improved weather, I felt comfortable taking my first official watch. The fellows also felt comfortable and went below for much-needed rest. I loved being at the helm in the middle of nowhere, watched over by more stars than I'd ever seen. The overwhelming vastness of the setting and the sounds of the boat rhythmically riding the waves intimidated me. I felt as though I was experiencing a spiritual phenomenon that was way beyond my comprehension.

I had time to think of a lot of things, including Bobbie. We never saw her. She would sneak out of her hiding place like a little mouse and stock up on food and drink when no one was around. Given what we had gone through, I wondered about her psychological state. No one discussed the fact that she intentionally isolated herself, and fortunately no one else chose to do the same, as she had the only private space on the boat.

By morning the wind had completely died. I heard Bobbie playing her guitar and assumed she must be okay. The rest of us relaxed. We swam off the boat, dried our clothes in the sun, and let the boat drift. At about noon Marv spotted a freighter. I was delighted when Sam, given his quasi-navigational skills, immediately went below to contact the freighter to establish our bearings. Unfortunately, he was unsuccessful in contacting the ship. A little later, we spotted two more freighters and realized we were crossing a shipping lane. Our efforts to contact these two ships also failed, and we concluded the obvious: The radio no longer worked. More bad news followed. Although we—except maybe for Bobbie—had been frugal with our use of water, we discovered one of the two tanks was almost empty, and had to assume we had a leak. But having survived the harrowing storms, we dismissed these negatives as minor problems.

The following day, Marv made French toast for breakfast, and I fixed a dinner: pork chops, applesauce, baked potatoes, peas, and, for dessert, cottage cheese with peaches. Nothing burned.

The wind picked up, and we headed south at a nice clip; at least I think we were heading south. Although we had no clear idea of where we were, we downplayed our loss of radio contact. Gathering clouds blocked the sun and then deleted the starry sky, turning our celestial navigational screen black. Below deck, I noticed the needle of the compass jumping around. The Bermuda Triangle was living up to its reputation of disregarding the earth's magnetic field.

We'd been gone a week. Although Sam had assumed that by this time we would have reached Saint Thomas, that prediction was less accurate than the psychic's forecast of my taking a trip over water in October.

Our reprieve from the gale-strength winds had clearly ended. By morning the swells were just as high as they had been a few days earlier, and the winds were unforgiving. Clearly, we had gone through the eye of the storm and were meeting it on the other side. According to Sam and Marv, our course was just to stay afloat. Which direction we headed was irrelevant. Because it was next to impossible to sleep, nobody was rested, and it became increasingly difficult for me to juggle shifts. I continued to stay up with whoever was at the helm and functioned on virtually no sleep.

Invariably, Paul got the most harrowing watches. He was nervous and edgy and, to our nonmedical crew, seemed on the verge of a nervous breakdown. The rest of us—excluding Bobbie—discussed whether we should talk to him about his condition. In the end, because there wasn't much we could do, we decided to pretend he was okay. He dedicated himself to tracking our course, even though we had no idea where we were. But it gave him something to do and kept his mind occupied. I looked over his shoulder to read his latest description of the weather: "too bad to describe."

Marv and Sam agreed to share the night shifts as Paul was in no condition to do so. The ship continued to mount the walls of water and slide spasmodically down the other side. At times when we were in the valley of water, I'd look up at a towering wave and wonder whether it might be the one to swallow the boat whole. Marv almost went overboard. Disco lightning framed him as he was swept from his perch. When the lightning flashed again, I saw his hands gripping the helm as though his life depended on it.

Forty-eight hours later the weather began to behave itself. We took inventory of what hadn't washed overboard. I tried to find some dry clothes to change into but gave up and left the soaked ones on.

That night, when I was aft with Paul, we spotted a ship but weren't sure it had seen us. I roused Marv and Sam, and we all aimed flashlights on our sails in hopes of being seen. Ten minutes later the ship's flashing lights let us know we had been. The ship passed within half a mile of our starboard side and disappeared: too close for comfort.

Again we were sure the storms were a thing of the past, but around 4:00 the following afternoon, another one hit. I couldn't believe the weather was so unrelenting. Continually running through my mind was the mantra, *"It has to end, it has to end!"* We were all exhausted, too tired to talk. We functioned like zombies, with telepathy replacing charades as our language. It was all I could do to make peanut butter and jelly sandwiches.

By morning the schizophrenic weather was improving. The screeches and moans of the *Fantasy* became whimpers. After going below for a much-needed nap, Sam returned to announce that the automatic pilot was out; the boat would have to be steered manually at all times.

Shortly after midnight, Marv and I saw a collection of lights. Thinking we might be near land, I got Sam up. After he took a quick look, he clattered down the ladder and turned on the Fathometer. It kept jumping around. Terrified that we might run aground, we came about and retraced our course. Ten minutes later we turned off the motor and just sat. By now Paul had joined us, and the four of us sat aft, guessing at what we might be looking at. We were sure it was not a ship; the lights, which kept popping on and off, had no order, and there were no green and red lights to indicate the ship's direction. Additionally, the span of the lights was so extensive we knew that it had to be larger than a super tanker. We concluded it must be land and decided to sit out the night watching and waiting.

Sam went below to check the Fathometer, thinking the jumpy readings might have been registering large schools of fish instead of shallow water. When he returned, he reported that the Fathometer was no longer functioning at all.

Toward morning the lights began to disappear, and by dawn the entire scene had evaporated. We were all perplexed as we looked toward the horizon and saw nothing but water. It was eerie. We had no idea where we were. We did know that we were running out of drinking water, which by now had become a real concern. The broken Fathometer and dysfunctional autopilot added layers of inconvenience, but were manageable. Our biggest problem was no radio communication.

When we spotted another freighter, I suggested that although we couldn't hear them, maybe they could hear us. Sam tried radioing and within seconds received a flashing light in response. He quickly asked yes and no questions to locate our latitude and longitude: one flash meant yes; two, no. As the freighter escaped from us, the ship's beacon of light circled a couple of times to signal farewell. We were ecstatic. I don't know why none of us had thought about testing for a return signal sooner, but we hadn't. Our location was 50 to 75 miles north of Puerto Rico, with longitude between 65 and 66 degrees.

The next day the weather was relatively calm. I changed into clothes I had previously committed not to wear until they were washed. Marv remarked that my bruised arms looked like very ripe bananas. It was clear I would have those souvenirs for some time to come.

At about 5:00 a.m. on day fifteen, Sam and I thought we smelled land, and at 11:30 we spotted it. We fell over each other trying to see whether we could figure out where we were on the topographic map. As the shoreline of Saint Thomas became clearer, we kept changing our guesses. A leaf floated by, and dolphins swam around the boat to check on us. What initially had looked like a fake backdrop became greener and more real.

Going around the west end of the island, we ran into short seas. After a seaplane crossed in front of us, we sailed across its runway and docked the boat. Given the strenuous exercise of changing sails in gale winds, it was not surprising that each of the fellows had lost 12 to 15 pounds. Sam looked like a skeleton.

Paul went off in search of his girlfriend, who had flown down from Wisconsin days earlier to meet him. Taking a shower was on the top of my list. Sam went to wash clothes. Marv stayed behind to tell Bobbie that she should go to a hotel, as she had not participated as part of the group; he told us later that she understood. That evening the rest of us celebrated.

Exhausted, we returned to the boat early. I slept for a few hours and then went up on deck. I lit my first cigarette in over two weeks and was enjoying the peace and quiet when Marv came up and joined me. He asked, "Can you give me a good reason why you're smoking that cigarette?"

I told him I could give him a few reasons, but I wasn't sure if any of them were "good" reasons. After pausing I added, "Maybe this is the last cigarette I'll ever smoke."

They say to succeed at giving up a bad habit you should do it at a significant time—a birthday, New Year's, the birth of a child. I knew I would never have another opportunity that would come close to matching the experience we had just been through and decided then and there that I would give up cigarettes for good. For all practical purposes, I have. During the last 40 years I have smoked seven cigarettes; each time it has been during a hurricane or typhoon.

With communication re-established, we learned that after we left Beaufort, friends on shore heard over the radio that we were heading directly into the path of a tropical storm. When they were unsuccessful in contacting us by radio, they had tried chasing us for two hours before giving up. They also told us that Tropical Storm Hallie had merged with another frontal zone and had become "extra tropical." This did not strike us as being news, as we had lived it. The Canadian boat that left the same time we did was thought to be lost at sea. That was news and made us realize once again how lucky we were to have survived.

Two years after our voyage, Sam was still sailing around the Caribbean. One day he returned to find his boat ablaze. He had left a crystal bowl on the wooden counter. The bowl had served as a prism for the sun to shine through and start the fire. He stood by helplessly as he watched our *Fantasy* disappear.

KEYS TO MEMORIES

Some of the hotel keys from my 1970s collection

I didn't start out stealing hotel keys. The idea came to me while I was unpacking from a trip to Latin America for work. There, mixed in with my rumpled clothing, were three hotel keys. Initially I was appalled, but these feelings quickly dissipated when I had an epiphany. Because most keys included the hotel's name and location, I thought,

"Why not collect keys to help me lock memories into place?" At the time I traveled so much I would sometimes wake up in the morning and literally wonder, "Where in the world am I?"

Yes, I took books of matches to help me remember where I'd been, but the idea of collecting keys seemed much more original. Many of the keys were fairly generic, others decorative, and some quite heavy. The brass key from the Ashoka Hotel in New Delhi weighed one pound four ounces. In the 1970s and '80s, there were no cards to slide through the slots on hotel-room doors.

I was brought up to never take anything that didn't belong to me, and although I lived by this tenet, with a little effort I was able to justify that I wasn't actually stealing the keys. After all, many honest people inadvertently walked away with hotel keys and never returned them. A final rationalization for my collecting keys was that such a hobby was appropriate for someone with the name Keekee.

Criteria for my new hobby included not taking keys from hotels I didn't like; not taking more than one key from the same hotel—unless by accident; and, although not a specific criterion, I often didn't bother keeping keys that were not artistically interesting or in some way distinctive. I would also return a key if hotel staff pursued me to an airport to retrieve it.

I confess that over the years I did experience a little guilt, and on occasion was tempted to follow the directions printed on many of the key tags: "If taken away please drop in nearest mailbox—postage guaranteed." But in the end, I resisted the temptation to do so. Now, decades later, not only is the guilt gone, but I assume many of the hotels, along with their keys, are also gone. I think of the dozens of keys I now possess as antiques that I had the foresight to collect decades ago.

Recently I sorted through my collection to see what memories might surface. Some of them stayed hidden in the subconscious: the Hotel Teranga in Dakar, Senegal; El Pardo Hotel in Lima, Peru; the Wentworth Hotel in Sydney, Australia. So although I had collected hotel keys to lock memories into place, clearly some locks had rusted over time. But others did bring back memories. I selected a few of the keys dating back to when I worked for Planned Parenthood.

Papua New Guinea

A black cracked-plastic key tag with "Budget Rent a Car" on one side and "Outrigger Motel, Vanama Cresent Port Moresby P.N.G." on the other served as an electrode to spark the memory of my stay in Papua, New Guinea (PNG). A couple of years after the country gained complete independence from Australia in 1975, Carrie—my regional director based in Manila—and I went to PNG to review its Planned Parenthood program. Carrie kept telling me stories about cannibalism in the hinterland and joked that we two well-nourished females would be delicious ingredients in a human stew.

Before venturing outside the city, we were advised that if we were in an accident, running away was our best option. One of the stories recounted by locals concerned the minister of education, who had not run away and was attacked by cannibals. Although I accepted the gruesome story as being at least partially based on truth, I had a hard time believing it entirely. There seemed hardly enough traffic to worry about accidents; only recently had the country's first and only traffic light been installed in the capital, Port Moresby.

The country was still finding its own way, but the women I spoke with at the family-planning clinic knew exactly what they wanted: Depo-Provera, a hormonal contraceptive injected subcutaneously and lasting for months. I explained that Depo was still undergoing clinical trials and that our organization could only provide contraceptives approved by the U.S. Food and Drug Administration (FDA). Of concern was the possible side effect of infertility when the contraceptive was discontinued.

The women insisted that they were quite willing to take that risk; they didn't want any more children. When I suggested sterilization, they responded that cutting the body was not culturally acceptable. The response made me realize that although we provided assistance throughout the world, it was on our terms. I understood the political and ethical implications of why Depo should not be provided until it was approved by the FDA (which did happen in 1992, some fifteen years later), but the experience exemplified the reality that donors make up the menu of choices. The women gathered in the clinic clearly thought they should have some say in the choices being provided for them. I could also appreciate their point of view.

As we drove back to the hotel, I couldn't help but think of the irony of not wanting to cut the body while accepting the rumored story of cannibals in the hinterland attacking the minister of education.

Ethiopia

Another key memory of the late 1970s was when Lenny, my regional director in Nairobi, and I went to Ethiopia. The day before we were to fly in, the United States Agency for International Development (USAID) staff in Addis Ababa told us to delay our arrival: The "revolving revolution," as Lenny referred to it, had heated up. We flew in a few days later, after the situation became more stable.

We stayed at the Addis Ababa Hilton, which was almost empty. The program people we met with confirmed that the situation was very bad and that a few days before our arrival dozens of students had been killed not far from our hotel. No wonder the hotel had few guests.

The following evening, Lenny went to visit friends and I went to the theater. Having mistakenly arrived an hour early, I found that except for a few soldiers, the lobby was empty. One of the soldiers pawed through my purse before motioning me in the direction of the auditorium. Upon entering, I discovered the entire right section was filled with a large Russian delegation. Heads turned collectively in my direction and watched as I pondered where I might sit in the otherwise empty theater.

I selected a center seat in about the tenth row and acted as if I was not being stared at. After about five minutes, a few from the uniformed delegation ventured across the aisle and approached me. We exchanged pleasantries until other patrons started trickling into the auditorium. The uniforms then flowed back across the aisle and melted into a tapestry of human sameness.

The theme of the play was clearly political. Although I understood none of the dialogue, it seemed to be about how cooperation between Ethiopia and Russia profited both countries. I glanced across the aisle but could not read the impassive faces. What were they thinking? They all seemed so well behaved and harmless, not living up to their reputation of an aggressive threat to the world.

A few days later in the elevator, on our way to check out, I asked Lenny if we could swap keys, as his was in much better condition than mine. He knew of my dubious hobby, and after comparing the tan plastic keys with gold lettering, he agreed and we made the switch.

We checked out, and as we were leaving, two employees at the doors tried to block our getaway. "Sir, your key, your key?" Their request was almost a plea. I mumbled to Lenny, "I'll give you the key; let's give them the key," but Lenny seemed to think it was a matter of principle, although what principle was involved, I have no idea.

"I don't have your key! What would I want with your key?" Lenny's voice echoed in the lobby vacant of other guests. This response, coming from a tall, confident black American impeccably dressed in his customary safari attire, intimidated the employees. I felt as if I were on a movie set and Lenny was overacting. I looked back at the bewildered and frightened desk clerks. I was sure it was not an easy time for the staff in charge of running the all-but-empty hotel. Their looks told me a missing key might mean the loss of a job. But Lenny was determined and won. And so another key was added to my collection.

Nigeria

Although the nature of memory is selective and over time one generally remembers the good and erases the bad, there are exceptions. Some of my memories need no key. Marc, my regional director for West Africa, had made reservations at a decent hotel in Lagos. Unfortunately, when we arrived we learned that the staff had bribed away our rooms. We decided to go ahead with our plans and look for another hotel when we returned in the evening.

We hired a taxi to take us to a mission hospital that was a couple of hours away. Feelings of terror quickly replaced the disappointment of having our hotel reservations canceled. Possibly our driver thought he was impressing us with his ability to weave in and out of traffic at excessive speed, but his performance jerked us around and I found myself clutching the back of his seat. Marc, whose father was Nigerian, tried to get him to slow down, but his plea was ignored.

Although I didn't get a good look, we raced by a woman, nude from the waist up, who lay awkwardly on the side of the road. She looked dead, and when we returned some hours later, I saw the woman in the same position and knew she was.

Since Marc was half Nigerian, I thought finding another hotel upon our return would not be too difficult, but I was wrong! It was 2:30 in the morning when we finally found a place to collapse. Calling it a hotel was a stretch. Even though the cost was the going rate of a five-star hotel, I would have rated it a minus-two. The sheets on the bed were dirty, there were no towels, and the door didn't lock. As I looked around the room I was reminded of my hitchhiking days; days that belonged to a distant past. My standards had changed over the years, and I had become used to clean sheets and doors that locked. Although there was no key to not keep, the memory has stayed with me.

Philippines

There were seedy hotels and there were spectacular hotels, like the Manila Hotel in the Philippines. People referred to it as Imelda's Hotel. Imelda was the wife of the Philippine president, Ferdinand Marcos, and was known for being extravagant. It was rumored that she owned more than 3,000 pairs of shoes.

As I made my way through the brightly lit lobby, with chandeliers suspended from the high ceiling, I felt elegant. After registering at the reception desk, I was presented with a key. The tag was an understated brass oval with "Manila Hotel" in flowing black script. The bellboy ushered me to my room, where there was not only the customary fruit but also stationery and matchbooks with my given name, Katharine, printed on them.

I smiled to myself, remembering that a few hours before my regional staff had met me at the airport with placards reading, "Welcome Katharine Minor." It was my first trip to Manila. I pulled Carrie aside and asked, "Why are you using the name Katharine instead of Keekee? You know I never use Katharine."

She laughed. "Here in the local language, Tagalog, *kiki* means 'vagina.' Not spelled the same but pronounced the same." Needless to say, on return visits to the Philippines, I have gone by Katharine.

Mauritius

Along with two others, I was hired as a consultant by the USAID to evaluate family-planning programs in a number of countries. When I arrived in Washington for the customary face-to-face briefing, I learned the itinerary had been changed for reasons of safety. The first program to be reviewed was now Mauritius. I had no idea where it was, but I wasn't about to confess my ignorance to those sitting around the briefing table.

Last-minute details kept me from locating Mauritius on a map before we left the following morning. When we changed planes in Nairobi, I thought to myself, Mauritius must be in Africa. It was night when we landed and took a taxi to the La Pirogue Hotel. The key, anchored to an eleven-ounce dark-gray stone, had the number 16 etched into it. In the moonlight, I could make out thatched roofs, but it wasn't until the next morning that I realized the hotel was located right on the beach.

When I arrived at the family-planning office, I requested a number of documents, including annual reports, bylaws, a list of staff, an organizational chart, budgets, minutes of board meetings, and so on. I ended by casually—and I thought somewhat cleverly—asking for a map. Staff brought me the materials and then left so I could review them in private. The first thing I looked at was the map, and there it was: Mauritius, an island. Unfortunately the water surrounding it was not identified.

A characteristic of my dyslexia is a poor sense of direction, so I have adjusted to having only a vague, and sometimes not very accurate, idea of where I am much of the time. I knew I was on an island and that was enough. I continued on with the evaluation and kept my ignorance to myself.

But I was curious. Leaving the country, I located a map in the seat pocket of the plane and learned that Mauritius was about seven hundred miles east of Madagascar in the Indian Ocean.

India

When I served as a Peace Corps volunteer in Bombay during the mid-1960s, I fantasized that someday I would return as a guest of the Taj Hotel. Back then I sometimes had tea in the Sea Lounge, located in the hotel. It served as a periodic retreat from the reality of living in the slums of Bombay. I would always try to sit next to a window so I could watch the shuffling of valet parking at the foot of the Gateway of India and observe ships sitting comfortably in the harbor. Inside the lounge I would occasionally be privileged to see a marriage in the making. Most marriages were arranged, and I enjoyed watching prospective brides and grooms exchange shy glances while their families chatted away.

Decades later, when I registered for my fantasy, I was handed a brass hexagonal-shaped key with red lettering. Per my request, I was given a room in the old section, built in the early 1900s. It was quieter and decorated with the past, whereas the new wing, added in the 1970s, was light and airy and bustled with activity. In the newer section, it was hard for me to imagine that I was in India. The lobby had a rich and international feel. Arabs in flowing white garb glided across the smooth marble floors, and wealthy Indians rushed about importantly.

Upon entering my assigned room, I went directly to the sink and turned on the water. It was magical. I thought back to my Peace Corps days and knew that in many parts of the city, water still only came at certain times of the day. Returning to the present, I felt guilty as I took an ever-so-brief shower.

My room faced the sea and the Gateway of India. Like a magnet, the view pulled me out of my room. I descended to the streets of Bombay, where the smells, the heat, the noise, and the throngs of people would trigger old memories and create new ones.

Some memories survive because they percolate to the surface of consciousness when recounted over the years. Others are brought to life because they are in some ways atypical. Still others survive because of their emotional intensity. All three categories exemplified the memories I had of my Peace Corps experiences in India a decade earlier. In many ways I felt as though I was returning home.

A CHANGING CHINA

*I join the parade celebrating the newly elected Chinese
Communist Party leadership, August 1977*

My first trip to China coincided with the Eleventh
Congress of the Chinese Communist Party, held in
Peking (Beijing) in August 1977. Chairman Hua replaced
Chairman Mao, who had died the previous September. I
arrived on the second day of a three-day parade celebrat-
ing the ushering in of new party leadership and putting

a stamp on the end of the Cultural Revolution. A stream of buses and trucks packed with workers from factories and communes kept arriving, allowing an estimated five to seven million people from the surrounding areas to take part in the parade. Because almost everyone was in the parade, there were few spectators, and aside from a sprinkling of tourists, everybody looked the same, with short black hair, dark pants, and white shirts.

After checking into the old section of the Peking Hotel, I too joined the parade. As I walked to Tiananmen Square, a short distance from the hotel, martial music competed with Chinese announcements booming from speakers and punctuated by firecrackers going off in all directions. Tiananmen Square was packed to capacity, and I was thrilled to watch history in the making. That night I fell asleep listening to the sounds of the parade; the following morning I woke up to the sounds of the parade.

I was part of a twenty-two member family-planning study group made up primarily of Planned Parenthood board members and staff. Our group was treated exceptionally well because of our sincere interest in learning about China's birth-planning program. Although their approach to family planning was being criticized in the West because of its draconian abortion policy, its leaders were determined to get the country's population growth under control. Their rationale was that the country could only feed so many people. Caring for those already here was the priority.

Our well-organized itinerary included Peking, Nanking, Yangchow, Soochow, Shanghai, and Canton. Each morning our group collected in the hotel lobby to receive instructions for the day from one of our interpreters. Our schedules were spandex tight, as if our hosts thought some of us might wander off and meet with unauthorized individuals. Actually, I might have, but I didn't speak Mandarin. The interpreters were keen on improving their English and asked for expanded definitions of words, or had one of us repeat a word so they could pronounce it better.

Because our primary purpose was to learn more about China's family-planning program, we visited hospitals and clinics, as well as communes and factories. Excluding pharmaceutical plants, most factories—sandalwood, jade, silk spinning, ceramics, lacquerware, embroidery—were traditional and used centuries-old skills. Major tourist sights—including the Great Wall, Ming Tombs, and the Forbidden City—were spliced into our itinerary. It was an exhausting schedule. For relaxation we attended a play and opera, both very political. None of us spoke Mandarin, and many in the group slept through the performances— not me, but I admit I was very bored. We did get to see a terrific acrobatics show, which required no translation.

Usually we traveled by private bus, but we flew from Peking to Nanking. Before embarking on the plane, we were weighed with our luggage, which I found disconcerting. I preferred traveling by bus. There was more to see, and traffic was usually light. Although there were community-owned trucks, public buses, and state-owned cars, I saw no private cars. Most of the population got around on generic black bicycles, which scattered to let buses through.

Communist Party officials greeted us at each location. After being ushered into a briefing room, we would sit in a semicircle with our hosts. Tea would be served, and although no one in our group smoked, small containers of cigarettes were always within reach. The rooms were simple and often decorated with poster-size portraits of Mao, Hua, Marx, Engels, Lenin, and Stalin. Those responsible for giving scripted presentations reminded me of telemarketers, and I listened carefully to hear whether any presenters went off message, which was seldom.

Discussions were open and informative. We were told that if someone became ill, trained medical personnel were always available, and if an illness was serious, a triage system was in place to accommodate emergencies. Patients could choose whether they preferred Western or Chinese medicine, or a combination.

Presenters genuinely tried to answer our questions but were often stumped when our queries were related to statistics. In these cases, the Gang of Four would be blamed. Members of this splinter group, led by Mao's late wife, had been accused of treasonous crimes and subsequently jailed the previous October, a month after Mao's death. The notorious group seemed to be the default reason for anything that had gone wrong.

Our hosts acknowledged that they expected changes in their script as a result of the recent Eleventh Congress meetings, but they had yet to receive instructions. The direction of certain policies seemed clear. A one-child policy was expected to take effect in the near future. Meanwhile, most communities we visited enforced guidelines dictating which couples would be permitted to have a child during a designated period of time.

Discussion of issues took place up and down the party hierarchy, with final decisions dictated by the Central Committee. Policies were then implemented throughout the country through a tightly monitored trickle-down system. Although those we met emphatically supported the wisdom of these policies, I knew that they had been carefully screened and cleared by the Communist Party. The party functionaries told us what they wanted us to hear, and showed us what they wanted us to see. They proudly described positive changes dictated by the party, such as the elimination of child labor and the tradition of binding women's feet. Elimination of the latter policy allowed women to become full partners in advancing social goals, bringing to life Mao's much-quoted slogan, "Women hold up half the sky." We were also reminded that we had seen no beggars, proof that everyone was being cared for.

Communist presenters endorsed their way of life as superior to that in the U.S. and did not question, at least in my presence, the wisdom of party leaders. This prompted me to ask why smoking, already proven to be unhealthful, wasn't forbidden. At first there was hesitation, and then the answer: most of the leaders smoked. This justification was followed by a comment that a policy was under consideration to forbid smoking by those who hadn't yet started.

Although there was a voiced consensus on most policies, there was less unanimity on questions regarding abortion. If a woman became pregnant without community approval, she would be counseled to have an abortion, and if she declined, persuasive counseling would continue until she agreed. When pressed, representatives admitted that in some cases counseling was not successful, resulting in a birth.

In only one location were we told that an unplanned newborn would be accepted into their community without consequences. In all other locations, if a couple disregarded the wishes of the community by having an unauthorized child, the couple was subjected to varying degrees of punishment. Examples given included less-desirable housing and work assignments, and fewer schooling opportunities for their children. In many instances no additional rations were provided for the unauthorized addition.

China's policy dictating who could have a child and when illustrates the philosophical difference existing between China and the United States. In China the needs of the society trumped those of an individual. As a result, individualism and creativity were sacrificed.

Although the Cultural Revolution had eliminated the need for higher education and sent the intelligentsia to the countryside, the education of children was a priority. At the locations we visited, the children appeared healthy and happy. They were neatly dressed in uniforms and so well behaved they looked like robots—happy little robots. The children clearly enjoyed performing for us, dancing and putting on little skits, which sometimes included a scene of the Gang of Four being destroyed.

The motto "Friendship First, Competition Second" was posted in school settings, and behavior that deviated from this philosophy was highly discouraged. So much attention was focused on children that I wondered whether they would be able to adjust to the hardships of adult life. But then, they were being raised in a carefully structured educational system specifically designed to prepare them for a prescribed future.

As part of a school's curriculum, children learned to exercise their eyes, a long-term useful skill. When we toured the Embroidery Research Institute in Soochow, we observed such detailed stitching that the finished pieces looked like photographs. To avoid eyestrain, employees— mostly women—stopped every two hours to rest and exercise their eyes. They also received mandatory eye exams every two years.

Children were taught low-level skills. I watched nine- and ten-year-olds cut each other's hair and observed children patiently filling containers of glue. Some might criticize the activities as exploiting the children, but in observing them, I thought they seemed to enjoy what they were doing.

At one school, a member of our group filmed children in a classroom and then immediately played it back for them. It was a magical moment. Etched in my memory are the awed, joyous expressions on the faces of the children, their teachers, and our interpreters as they saw themselves on film.

Regardless of the site—schools, factories, communes, or hospitals—the interpreters had no problem with our taking pictures, even in surgical settings. At the largest maternity hospital in Shanghai, we photographed a woman undergoing a tubal ligation and another, a cesarean section. In both instances acupuncture was used as the sole anesthesia. The patients smiled and waved to us as we peered down into the operating theater. The only time we were asked not to take pictures, and this was at the request of the patient, was when we observed a tubal ligation performed at the Peking Maternity Hospital.

The advantages of using acupuncture as an anesthetic were impressive. In all three surgeries, the women appeared to be in little or no pain as they conversed freely with their anesthesiologists. Acupuncture also has the advantage of not leaving behind a toxic drug trail, which the body then has to dispose of. In many ways, traditional Chinese medicine adheres more closely to the frequently quoted Hippocratic oath "First do no harm" than Western allopathic medicine, which relies heavily on pharmaceuticals.

The frank exchanges between our group and our hosts were sometimes lost in translation, but overall both groups learned from each other. The Chinese expressed surprise that women in America could not get abortions easily and that contraceptives were not free. The lives of workers were so closely monitored that not only were the production levels of employees posted publicly, but also the type of contraceptive being used by individual female employees!

When data were available, using the beginning of the Cultural Revolution as a benchmark, we were shown how production had increased in various factories. Statistics documenting the drop in the birthrate were also provided.

Not all Chinese citizens were enamored with the government's social policies. Although our time was tightly programmed and monitored, one evening we were able to meet privately with Chen Daisun, who had taught economics at Peking University for more than fifty years. He was encouraged by Chairman Hua's recent remarks declaring the Cultural Revolution officially over. In Chen's view, ten years of progress had been lost due to the Cultural Revolution's systematic closing of educational institutions and sending the intelligentsia to the countryside to work.

He was cautiously optimistic that the new congress would promote science and technology and reopen the institutions of higher learning.

*   *   *

When I returned to China eight years later, I could not believe how much the country had changed. As coordinator for new technology and training for the Association for Voluntary Sterilization (AVS), I had organized and secured private funding for a group of seven physicians from various countries to go to China and evaluate a no-scalpel vasectomy procedure developed there by Dr. Li Shunqiang. Based on their findings, they were to recommend whether the technique should be incorporated into curricula for physicians.

In the hospitals and clinics we visited, there was a generational gap between newly trained and older doctors. The gap in age coincided with the years of the Cultural Revolution. Whereas on my first trip presenters followed well-rehearsed scripts, the physicians we met on my return trips expressed their own opinions freely. They concurred with Professor Chen's assessment almost eight years earlier that precious time had been lost, and they were determined to catch up with the rest of the world, particularly in the area of technology.

The visiting physicians were very impressed with the no-scalpel vasectomy, and strongly advocated training in the technique. The procedure took about ten minutes, used local rather than general anesthesia, and had fewer complications than vasectomies performed using a scalpel. China certainly had sufficient experience in performing vasectomies. Between 1971 and 1984, over eleven million men had undergone vasectomies in Szechuan Province alone.

By 1986, China's one-child policy had been well established, and couples were understandably hesitant to choose sterilization as a contraceptive. They understood it was considered permanent, which meant that if their child died, they would not be able to have another. Other contraceptives were readily available, but because abortion was included in China's family-planning program, no funding was available from the United States government.

The lack of donor funding, coupled with many Chinese having reservations about sterilization, led to the selection of another country for training in the no-scalpel vasectomy technique. The following year, AVS, in collaboration with Thailand's Population and Community Development Association (PDA), sponsored training in Bangkok for physicians from a half-dozen countries. Today, the no-scalpel vasectomy procedure is performed widely throughout the world, and it is estimated that each year over half a million procedures are done in the United States alone.

As the Chinese physicians I spoke with years earlier had hoped, the country was leaping into the future with technological advances. Their economy soared even as the population continued to grow, increasing from approximately 944 million in 1977 to more than 1.376 billion in 2015. After thirty-seven years the Communist Party discontinued its one-child family policy in 2015, and as we move into the future, evaluating the impact of this policy will have less to do with population statistics than with the sociological consequences it created.

My experiences in China exemplify how quickly the world changes. China's transformation during the eight years between my visits over a quarter of a century ago continues to this day. A changing China serves to illustrate how those of us living longer lives not only have the opportunity to see history in the making, but with the extra years given to us, we have time and perspective to reflect on that history.

At the turn of the nineteenth century in the United States, the average lifespan was forty-seven years: long enough for people to get a snapshot of the world. Today we see the world as a fast-paced movie, with changes to the script being rewritten as events occur. Most of the scenes capture episodes of ongoing wars, how our food is being chemically altered to feed the world, and how man-made pollution is impacting our climate. Sometimes we are presented with previews of pandemics to come. Although the number of actors in this world movie has tripled in my lifetime, this major factor, responsible for contributing to the problems mentioned above, lacks much dialogue because of its political sensitivity.

I chose not to have children. Instead, I'm leaving behind words. Words don't consume the world's resources, they are well-behaved, and they don't leave a carbon footprint.

Peace Corps in the Marshall Islands

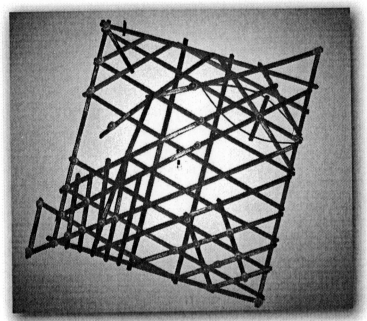

Map of the Marshall Islands, with shells denoting atoll

Tootling down the narrow road bisecting Majuro, the capital of the Marshall Islands, I kept imagining I was previewing the end of civilization. Typhoon Axel, the first typhoon to hit the Pacific atoll in 1992, arrived in January, one month after my arrival. The blanket of garbage it tossed over the island was accompanied by an inescapable stench. This was not an auspicious beginning for my two years as Peace Corps country director in the Republic of the Marshall Islands.

The Peace Corps had hired me to be its first country director for Bangladesh, and because one of my regional offices had been located there when I worked for Planned Parenthood, it was a country I knew something about. I was already in Peace Corps staff training when the Bangladeshis decided to postpone—for the fifth time—the start of a Peace Corps program. They wanted to wait until after their upcoming elections. When I interviewed for the position, I'd asked whether they were sure the Bangladeshis wanted the Peace Corps. On previous visits to the country, I'd spoken with government officials who questioned what volunteers could do that they could not, "except eat our food."

The timetable for opening a program in Bangladesh was put on hold, but since I was already in staff training, the Peace Corps administration asked whether I would consider another country. The Republic of the Marshall Islands was the next country where the position of country director needed to be filled, and I agreed to the switch. My first thought was that I could add it to my list of countries visited. My second thought was, where is it? I left the interview in search of a map.

The population of Bangladesh was more than 2,000 times that of the Marshalls, and as I mentally withdrew from the realities of Bangladesh, I began to fantasize about living on a sparsely populated island situated halfway between Hawaii and Guam and only a few degrees above the equator.

Getting meaningful information and a sense of the country wasn't easy. I did finally track down someone in the State Department who told me she didn't know much about the place but remembered receiving calls from men asking about going there to escape alimony.

The Marshalls had been included in the Federated States of Micronesia, part of the trust territories acquired by the United States at the end of World War II. In 1979 the Marshalls became self-governing and received sovereignty in 1986 as part of its compact agreement with the United States. In the agreement, the U.S. was to provide aid and defense of the islands in exchange for continued military use of the missile-testing range on Kwajalein. Between 1946 and 1958, the United States used the Marshalls as a nuclear testing site. Due to fallout, some islands remain uninhabitable to this day, and illnesses related to the testing continue to plague citizens of the country. Reparations paid by the U.S. amounted to more than a billion dollars, giving the Marshallese the distinction of receiving the largest per capita income of foreign aid from the U.S.

After training, I flew to Hawaii in a plane full of WWII veterans on their way to commemorate the bombing of Pearl Harbor fifty years earlier. Given the occasion, their celebratory mood felt a little incongruous. I sat between two veterans who became excited when they learned that I was on my way to the Marshalls. They had both been there during the war and raved about its beautiful lagoon. I thought of them two days later as I looked out the plane window just before landing in Majuro. The white beaches trimming the islands looked stunning and inviting, just as they had been described, but I soon learned that what I imagined as powdery white sand was jagged coral.

I timed my arrival to coincide with my birthday, December 7, thinking it would be a good way to launch the next couple of years of my life. I really didn't know what to expect, but I also didn't care; I was on a new adventure, and that was all that mattered.

In most countries, Peace Corps country directors have cooks and servants, perks I had looked forward to experiencing had I gone to Bangladesh, but there were no such perks in the Marshalls. The similarities between Bangladesh and the Marshalls started and ended with them both having too much, and too little, water. Much of Bangladesh floods when monsoon rains arrive, and the seventy square miles of islands making up the Marshalls are scattered over 750,000 miles of ocean. With climate change, the islands are now disappearing into the Pacific. A shortage of drinking water was a problem for both countries.

When I arrived, arranging for drinking water was at the top of my list. The proprietor in charge of delivering containers was German. He seemed a little crazy, and I thought—based on nothing but my imagination—he might be a former Nazi who had come to the Marshalls right after WWII to escape being tried for war crimes. Although the Nazi part was only in my head, the crazy part seemed justified as I watched him prance around in his bare feet while we set up a schedule for water deliveries.

Majuro was a small town, and it didn't take long for me to orient myself. After arranging for the delivery of water, I went to Reimers, one of the two general stores. A sign on the door read, "We have Body Bags." Not something you saw advertised every day. Toward the back of the store there was a grocery section. Seeing milk products initially delighted me, until I discovered the expiration date on a carton of cottage cheese was four months earlier. The fresh vegetables looked as though they had been salvaged from a garbage dump. My fantasy of finding fresh tropical fruit quickly faded.

Although I'd been able to arrange for drinking water, Typhoon Axel necessitated substantial rationing. The purpose of my "end of civilization" drive was to collect desalinated water from the American embassy for my Peace Corps volunteers, who fortunately were all on island for training, and safely stashed away in a hotel.

I felt a sense of exhilaration as I drove over the highest point of the island, a small bridge referred to as Mount Majuro, which towered 13 feet above sea level. I stopped by the weather station on my way to the embassy to see which islands had received the most damage, but postponed thinking about what changes might need to be made in volunteer assignments until after the storm damage could be assessed.

Water was important but so was finding suitable housing. My predecessor had not renewed the Peace Corps lease because he said the house he was living in was "falling apart." Instead, he made temporary arrangements for me to rent from Joe Murphy, who had served as a Peace Corps volunteer decades before and stayed on.

The window in my eight-foot-wide bedroom framed rusting cars. In the living area, there were small slits of windows positioned a few inches below the ceiling. Joe said their placement was intentional, allowing light in but set high enough so no one could see in. The place felt creepy. Sometimes when I woke up in the morning I would find the dank and musty living area littered with a gray film of dead winged insects—the remains of an all-night orgy. The unpleasantness of the place prompted me to make my housing a priority.

Two days after my arrival I phoned Jim Abernathy, an American who was overseeing the construction of the new capitol building as well as a couple of duplexes. He answered the phone rather abruptly and then apologized, explaining that he was really stressed out and that if he didn't get back to California for Christmas he would go "crazy." He proceeded to rattle off his list of frustrations, in particular the sinking of the foundation of the new capitol. He then launched into his own history, including the fact that his mother had married seven times. I might have attributed his ramblings to drink, but he sounded sober; maybe that was the problem. Eventually, we came around to my housing situation; he confirmed that he was building a couple of duplexes and said that he'd save one for me.

The drive to the embassy for water gave me the opportunity to check out where I would be moving once construction was completed. Although my bright-blue duplex wouldn't be ready for a few months, I knew it would be worth the wait. It was located right on the lagoon, with its foundation doubling as a seawall. Across the picturesque lagoon, islands underlined by white coral during low tide appeared to float at high tide. I, like most foreigners living on the island, wanted to face the water, while most Marshallese liked facing the road. With typhoons like Axel, I could understand their preference.

The Peace Corps office was no prize, but it was better than my initial housing. My Marshallese deputy told me the office had originally been a warehouse. He remembered that after World War II, his and other families would go there to collect food supplies provided by the U.S. Department of Agriculture (USDA). Palm trees felled by Typhoon Axel lay in front of the building, and water, which flooded the cement floor, shorted-out the equipment. I knew finding alternative office space would also become a priority.

The airport, initially closed because of flooding, opened within a week, allowing workers from the Federal Emergency Management Agency (FEMA) to arrive and assess the damage done by Axel. Most Peace Corps volunteers trickled back to their islands, with some serving as translators for FEMA workers. One volunteer went back to the States when she learned her straw hut had been blown away by the typhoon. Although I offered her the option of an alternate assignment, the storm's demolition of her hut gave her the excuse she wanted for early termination.

Peace Corps volunteers who make it through the first year usually stay and complete their assignments. By then, most volunteers have learned the language and adjusted to their living and working situations. Having reached the halfway mark, the countdown becomes easier, even for those who may not have been all that happy initially.

Island living was a lonely existence for many of the volunteers, whose numbers were only a fraction of what they had been when the Peace Corps first came to the islands in the 1960s. Radio stations were located on the islands where volunteers were placed, and served as my primary method of communicating with them. A conference call was scheduled for every Tuesday afternoon between five and five-thirty. Because it was over the radio, some Marshallese tuned in for entertainment; who wouldn't want to know if a volunteer had diarrhea? In addition to the weekly conference calls, if a volunteer had an emergency, scheduling to bring him or her into Majuro was also arranged via the radio.

The Peace Corps had been in the Marshalls almost thirty years, and although worldwide forty percent of volunteers still work in education, only in the Republic of the Marshall Islands and the remaining Federated States of Micronesia were they still serving as elementary school teachers. Part of the Peace Corps' mission is to help build infrastructure so that host-country nationals can step in and take over projects when volunteers leave. Unfortunately, most qualified Marshallese teachers had little interest in returning to their home islands and often left the country to teach elsewhere. The Marshallese seemed to think of the Peace Corps as one of their many entitlement programs, and assumed volunteers would continue to come and teach indefinitely.

Volunteers lived with families, who served as their social network in the community. For all practical purposes, my social life was limited to work. When I arrived, the American ambassador told me that he had never been invited to a Marshallese home. The only time I was ever invited was at the end of my first year, when the secretary of education invited me for Christmas dinner.

The night before that, Christmas Eve, a dog bit me. I went to the hospital, assuming I would need to go through a series of rabies shots. There I was told that no rabies existed on the island. So two pieces of good luck in two days: I didn't have to have rabies shots, and I had a nice

Christmas dinner with a Marshallese family. My biggest bit of luck, though, was when I took the American ambassador to a fundraiser and won the door prize...a trip to Bali! I truly felt I deserved it.

I arranged to join a tour when I got to Bali. When the friend who had organized it had to cancel because not enough people signed up, he suggested I contact the local tour guide he'd engaged for the group, Ratih Cokorda. I faxed her and asked whether she could meet me at the airport and make a hotel reservation for two nights. Our communication wasn't quite perfect. When she met me at the airport in a large van, I quickly realized that she expected to be my tour guide during my entire ten-day stay. Not only was there this big van, but she also had made child-care arrangements for her two-year-old daughter. I felt trapped. After some discussion, we agreed we would travel around in her little green truck: I would pay for the gas and a daily fee of $30.

I was so lucky to have been trapped. Everybody seemed to know Ratih, and we received special treatment. I soon learned she was a princess descended from royalty and a well-known *legong* dancer. Our touring around was punctuated by her well-attended performances, but it wasn't until I returned to the Marshalls that I fully understood just how famous she really was. There, in the capital's tiny tourist office, was a giant poster of a Balinese dancer—Ratih!

I can't say that after my two-week vacation I was delighted to get back to Majuro, where bars defined the social life of the community. I understood why, during my training, so many Peace Corps staff thought sending a woman to serve as a country director in the Marshalls was a really bad idea. Given my position, I did not feel comfortable hanging out in bars, and unless there was an official function, I spent most of my free time alone. If I received a cassette tape from someone back home, I might play it as I ate dinner. On weekends I usually went to the office.

Things were quiet, but I found observing life around me interesting. I had my hair cut at *Curl Up and Dye*, where the hairdresser snipped away under the watchful eye of his pet parrot, who remained perched on his shoulder the entire time. They made quite a pair. At an event hosted by the American ambassador for Americans living on the island, the hairdresser brought his parrot; the ambassador was not amused.

Although not much happened on the island, when it did, it made news. I had two volunteers with me when I picked up another at the airport. Because the volunteers did not get to Majuro often, one suggested we stop at the Thai Table to eat. As I pulled into a parking space, the sole of my flip-flop caught the gas pedal. Instead of stopping the truck, I slammed into a utility pole, which promptly fell over and landed on another truck.

I asked one of the volunteers to go find somebody who looked official. He found the manager, who came out and said not to worry about it: "Just go upstairs and have a drink." Another person came by and reiterated that I didn't have a thing to worry about. He tried to reassure me that because both the Peace Corps truck and the truck with the pole lying on it were government vehicles, insurance would cover everything.

At my insistence, someone not looking very official but willing to play the part finally arrived and took down my statement. The pole was moved off the truck and laid on the ground in the parking lot. There it remained for six weeks as an embarrassing reminder. Although I was not named when the account of the accident was printed in the entertainment section of the paper, everybody on the island knew who was responsible.

One Sunday upon leaving the office, I realized that I had locked the ignition key inside the Peace Corps truck and I did not have a spare. The office was not far from the police station, so I walked over and asked for assistance. Twenty minutes later four men appeared, more than the number needed for the task, but then again it was Sunday morning and things were quiet. Things were always quiet Sunday mornings, as they followed Saturday nights, which invariably flowed with liquor into the wee hours of the morning.

As we walked back to the truck, I chatted with Frank, one of the three men not in uniform. He said that when he was younger he had gone through the Job Corps, a free education and training program that supports helping young people learn a career or earn a high school diploma. I was sure he had a story, but asked, "So have any of you ever broken into a car before?"

"No." Frank answered. "They sent the wrong prisoners." It was then that I realized I was about to give "on-job training" to convicts. I felt uneasy as I instructed the three prisoners how to use coat hangers to jimmy the locks. Meanwhile, the uniformed policeman sat casually on the seawall nearby.

There was very little chance that any of the prisoners would try to escape. Where could they go? Although Majuro was the largest atoll, it was still just a collection of islands. After thanking the prisoners for our successful break-in, I watched them saunter back to jail. I thought of my life as not being that different from theirs. The walls that guarded all of us were made of water, stretching to the horizon in every direction.

As I thought about how isolated we all were, I was reminded of the time I flew with an ill volunteer from the Marshalls to Hawaii. It was Halloween night. Actually, it was the second Halloween night that year: the Marshalls sat on the international date line, and the flight to Honolulu crossed back over that line. The flight took as long as one from New York to London.

Did I like being so isolated, living a few degrees above the equator in the middle of nowhere? A better question: was I glad I made the decision to go to the Marshalls? The answer is, "Yes."

My career in population and family planning had taken me to places overloaded with people, and although during the time I was in the Marshalls it had one of the highest growth rates in the world, by comparison, it was uncluttered by people. I adjusted to being by myself much of the time, deciding I wasn't that hard to live with. As always, although my experiences of living on a tropical island didn't match my initial fantasy, I appreciated and valued the opportunity to experience another culture. Mother Nature provided entertainment, not only with exciting weather, but with clear night skies filled with stars, and lots of water for reflection.

When I lived in the Marshalls, two people sent me the same clipping from *The New York Times* stating that due to rising seas, the Marshalls might disappear in thirty years. That was over twenty years ago, and recent articles point to this prediction becoming a reality. As the country disappears into a rising ocean, I can't help but wonder whether my memories will last longer than the country itself.

Reflections

The adage that it takes a village to raise a child is an apt analogy to the writing of this memoir. Because I'm dyslexic, the idea of writing a book was not something I gravitated to easily, but with the arrival of the personal computer and spell-check, coupled with the encouragement of friends, I took on the task. When I took courses at the Bethesda and Chautauqua writers' centers to work on individual pieces, I was often asked, "Who's your audience?" I usually responded that since I'm not leaving behind children, it was a record for family and friends. But over time I began to think of the project as being primarily for myself.

When I initially started writing, I relied on my once-excellent memory, but as I've aged, my memory—along with my hearing and eyesight—has diminished. I wanted the stories to be as accurate as possible, so I dug up my travel journals. Reading through them not only brought back long-forgotten details, but also allowed me to relive and enjoy the experiences without the initial effort—I no longer hitchhike with a forty-pound pack on my back.

In addition to my journals, I also tracked down friends who were with me on various segments of my travels. I asked them to read through pieces and verify that what I was recording was consistent with their memories. This approach for accuracy proved rewarding in other ways. For example, I contacted Deborah Oakley, who had been on the China trip in 1977. I had not seen or talked to her in thirty-five years, but I knew she had taught nursing at the University of Michigan. I googled the site and learned that although she had retired, an email address was listed for her. I wrote immediately, and within fifteen minutes she responded, stating she would be delighted to read it. She added that she and her husband were in Mexico and had an extra room, so why didn't I come down? I did the following year, and we had a wonderful reunion.

Reliving my experiences with friends and reading my journals reminded me of how lucky I was to still be alive. When I was young, I was too immersed in life to think about death. Obviously at the time I knew I was taking risks, but I liked living on the edge. As I've gotten older, the edge has gotten duller. My body reminds me that I've had my fun and it's now time to slow down and act my age, as if I had a choice. In recent years I have gone to India for Ayurvedic treatments, designed to keep the body in balance with herbs and oils. I try to keep active, but I define "active" differently than I did decades ago.

Clearly, as I stack up the years, my priorities have changed. I now budget energy more than time or money, and I think of writing as an age-appropriate activity. Although when I was younger I felt I had to experience life directly, I am now happy to rely more on technology. I appreciate the fact that I can listen to books on CDs, watch TV, and connect to the world via my computer.

But experiencing the world through technology is not the same as living it. Not only is the information processed through the person or persons recording the information, but the senses also get cheated. There have been many technological advances, particularly in perfecting visuals over the years, but in watching a film one can only imagine smells, tastes, heat, humidity, and unfiltered sounds. Fortunately for me, my travel employed all five senses, and in some cases a sixth sense.

From my standpoint, the timing of my life has been excellent. The technological inventions during my tenure here on earth have been rapid and plentiful. They have served to make the world much smaller, which brings me to my concern about the increasing population. It's hard for me to believe that the population has already tripled in my lifetime. Every day we hear stories about shortages of food, water, oil, etc., but seldom do we hear or think about the cause: too many people. I realize that wars, famine, and natural disasters have been with us for millennia, but in today's world, it is the consequences of overpopulation that I worry about. People are coming into the world at a faster rate, and many of us are hanging around longer. In the U.S., at the end of the nineteenth century, the average life span was 47 years; today it is around 76 for men and 80 for women. This means that for those of us living longer, we have the opportunity to observe how our lives become history.

I was born two years to the day before the bombing of Pearl Harbor, so I even remember the end of World War II. My family was celebrating at the Selman Field officers' club, where my father, Major Minor, allowed me to order as many Cokes as I wanted. More vivid memories include landing on the moon (not me), the Kennedy assassinations, and the terrorist attack on 9/11. The purpose of this book has been to record a more personal history.

Although I'm not yet finished with making memories, we all eventually run out of life, and I wanted to make sure I completed this book before it was too late. For those of you who keep thinking about writing a book, I say, "Do it." But the motivation should not be for money, but rather for all the gratifying experiences that become incorporated into the process.

Looking back, I feel extremely fortunate that although I have no formal degree from the school of international travel, my odyssey has taught me more about the world and its people than I ever learned in an academic setting.

Acknowledgments

As alluded to earlier, it took a village to write this book. In appreciation, I'd like to mention some of its most helpful citizens. Carla Wright, a roommate from college, was persistent in encouraging me to write my travel experiences. I'm not sure the experiences would ever have turned into words on pages had it not been for her nudging me over the decades and providing invaluable help with editing suggestions. Anne Williams, from Peace Corps days, provided not only useful editing and contextual comments, but she also had a talent for identifying mistakes. Cathy Melocik added her professional expertise to the editing process. Her efforts were followed by Ellen Ewens, whom I initially met on the *Experiment in International Living* in 1960. Diane Brown, who recently retired as the book editor for AARP was the next editor to volunteer to read the manuscript. And last but not least, Shelli Klein, also a recently retired copy editor, provided a final review. (A dyslexic can't have too many editors as there are plenty of errors to go around.)

Editing was not the only area in which I relied on the skills of others. Bob Cole used his professional skills to digitize old slides for the pictures in the book, and provided invaluable assistance (I helped) for the cover. Ruth Porter, a friend from high school who I reconnected with after more than fifty years, has authored a few books and therefore was able to give me many publishing tips as well as unending encouragement.

Travel companions who read relevant sections for accuracy include Muryl Anderson, Anne Sarich, Deborah Oakley, and Abett Icks. Others who provided useful suggestions include Phil Safford, Mike and Terry McGee, Maryland Cole, Kristin Kovaci, June Lunney, Jill Sandler, and Jim and Jane Mead.